The Simple 6™
for
Beginning Writers

Prompts and Activities
Grades K-2

Kay Davidson

Pieces of Learning

D1262101

CLC0408
ISBN 978-1-931334-97-6
© 2007 Pieces of Learning

Dedication

To Kaylin and Dawson Kieft, the next generation of Simple 6™ writers.

Acknowledgements

Many thanks to all the teachers who provided personal input and student writing samples; with special thanks to my colleagues and friends from:

School City of Mishawaka

South Bend Community School Corporation

Caston School Corporation

Fairfield Community Schools

Concord Community Schools

Elkhart Community Schools

John Glenn School Corporation

Porter Township School Corporation

Southwest School Corporation

To Kathy Balsamo, my editor, and the rest of The Pieces of Learning Family

Table of Contents

Chapter 1:   Using Picture Books as a Motivation
                    for Writing 5-6
            K-2 Writing Standards 7-9
            The Value of Reading to Your Students Every Day 10
            Teaching The Simple 6™ as You Read to Your Class...11
            Quick Reference Guide for K-2 Students 12
            As You Read Aloud to Your Class: 15 Ideas..........13-15
            Read Aloud Recommendations 16-29
            Your Top 10 Picture Book Choices for Read Alouds....30
            Getting the Most out of a Picture Book 31

Chapter 2:   Teaching Young Students to Draw.....................33
            Books for Motivating Students to be Artists...........34
            Drawing Picture Book Characters with Young Writers ..35
                    Pigeon...39
                    Maisy 41
                    Arthur 43
                    Lyle 45
                    Spot 47
                    Chrysanthemum (Lilly) 49
                    Clifford...52
                    Other Favorites..................................54-60

Chapter 3:   Assessment for Beginning Artists and Authors 61
            Assessment Across the District 62
            Assessment in the Classroom 64
            Defining Expectations for Beginning Writers
                    in Your School 65-67
            Tracking Progress in K-2...............................68-72
            Scoring Kindergarten Writing/Drawing Samples 73-75
            KDG: Baseline Expectations
            Prompt: Me/Anchor Papers 76-82
            Expectations Throughout the Year 83
            Prompt: My Home/1st Semester Anchor Papers 84-91
                            2nd Semester Anchor Papers 92-97
            Scoring Student Writing/Drawing Samples
                    in Grade 1 98
            GR 1: Baseline Expectations 98

Prompt: My Family/Anchor Papers 99-106

Expectations Throughout the Year 107

Prompt: My Fun Day/1st Semester Anchor Papers 108-115

         2nd Semester Anchor Papers......116-121

GR 2: Baseline Expectations 122

Prompt: Being a Good Friend/Anchor Papers 123-130

Moving into Formal Assessment During the

    Second Semester 131

The Simple 6™ Poster 132

Chapter 4: The Simple 6™: A Writing Rubric for Kids 133

What is The Simple 6™? 134

Review of the Components 135

The Rubric 137

Implementing The Simple 6™ Writing Program 138

Nine Week Overview 139

Tips for Success 141

Using the Simple 6™ to Guide and Assess

    Writing-only Prompts 142

The Simple 6™ Quick Reference Chart 143

Mini Rubrics 144

Class Analysis Chart 145

Quarterly Assessment Packet 146-149

Prompt and Anchor Papers 150-155

Quarterly Tracking Chart 156

Yearly Class Record 157

Chapter 5: Prompts for Beginning Writers 159

Kindergarten Assessment Packet 161-164

Prompts for Kindergarten Students 165-177

Grade 1 Assessment Packet 178-181

Prompts for Grade 1 Students 182-194

Grade 2 Assessment Packet 195-198

Prompts for Grade 2 Students

        1st Semester: with drawing 199-211

        2nd Semester: without drawing ..212-224

Picture Book Resources 225

Chapter 1: Using Picture Books as a Motivation for Writing

K-2 Writing Standards

The Value of Reading to Your Students Every Day

Teaching The Simple 6™ as You Read
to Your Class

Quick Reference Guide for K-2 Students

As You Read Aloud to Your Class: 15 Ideas

Read Aloud Recommendations

Your Top 10 Picture Book Choices for Read Alouds

Getting the Most out of a Picture Book

Chapter 1: Using Picture Books as a Motivation for Writing

When I first started teaching, kindergarten's focus was readiness – getting students *ready* to follow rules, getting *ready* to get along with one another, and getting *ready* to become independent workers. They learned how to use lined and unlined paper, how to hold a fat pencil or crayon, how to color, and how to use scissors properly. Somewhere down the road they learned the colors, how to sing the alphabet song, and how to count to 20. This preparation helped ensure that all students were *ready* to go to first grade . . . *ready* to conquer the cognitive skills . . . *ready* to begin learning how to read and write.

During the past decade, state standards and national guidelines have drastically raised the level of academic expectations for young students, especially those in kindergarten. The development of gross and fine motor skills, creative play time, nap time, and "learning how to go to school" time, as well as Piaget's research on developmental readiness, are no longer the curricular focus. The kindergarten day is now filled with the three Rs – Reading, 'Riting, and 'Rithmetic.

Primary students have always come in all shapes, all sizes, and all ability levels. However, students are now coming to kindergarten at levels *so* diverse that it is almost impossible for teachers to meet all the academic expectations – not to mention the social skills. There is also a growing number of young non-English speaking students coming to school. Add to that the assumption that all those *readiness* skills were mastered in day care, home care, or preschool. Early primary teachers, especially kindergarten teachers, are stressed to the max!

Academic standards now dictate what is to be taught at each specific grade level, and state assessments are designed to test mastery of those skills. While each state's format is different, the expectations are similar. Becoming familiar with the standards at your grade level is now imperative. Designing themes, units, and lessons around those standards is logical and necessary. On the other hand, having to *create* a list of the standards taught and/or mastered on a daily basis is a critical waste of instructional time.

What do your state standards tell you about the expectations for writing? If you were asked to list them and discuss how your students are progressing, could you do it? Some states' formats are more cumbersome than others' are. The key to *knowing* your standards is to break them down into short sentences or phrases that clearly tell you what is expected. Organize them all on 1 page so you can refer to them as you plan instructional strategies.

Based on Indiana's Academic Standards for Language Arts, following is a guide for organizing your standards on one page. Fill in the blanks with other standards that may be required by your state. Then retype your list, laminate a copy, and put it somewhere on your desk where it is easily accessible.

Kindergarten Writing Standards

Writing Process
Discuss ideas for stories.
Dictate a story.
Write a story with pictures, letters, or words.
Draw a picture about a specific topic.
Write a story about a specific topic.

_____
_____
_____
_____

Listening and Speaking
Speak in complete sentences.
Describe people, places, and things.
Tell a story in logical order.

_____
_____
_____
_____

Language Conventions
Write capital and lower case letters.
Share ideas in complete sentences.

_____
_____
_____
_____

SOCIAL FOCUS FOR PROMPTS: Me / My Family

Grade 1 Writing Standards

Writing Process
Discuss ideas for writing.
Use a planning strategy.
Write stories that tell about personal or imaginary experiences.
Write stories that describe or explain.
Use descriptive words.
Revise writing.

_____

_____

_____

_____

Listening and Speaking
Stick to the topic when speaking.
Tell about experiences in logical order.
Use descriptive words.
Retell stories.
Restate simple two-step directions.

_____

_____

_____

_____

Language Conventions
Write in complete sentences.
Use end marks correctly.
Capitalize the first word in a sentence.
Capitalize names and I.

_____

_____

_____

_____

SOCIAL FOCUS FOR PROMPTS: Me / My Family / My Friends

Grade 2 Writing Standards

Writing Process
Discuss ideas for writing.
Stick to the topic as you write.
Use a planning strategy to organize ideas.
Find ideas for writing in books and pictures.
Write stories that tell about personal or imaginary experiences.
Write stories that describe or explain in detail.
Write with a beginning, a middle, and an end to your stories.
Use descriptive words.
Write a friendly letter.
Revise to improve order.
Revise to improve sentence structure.
Revise to include more detailed descriptions.

_____

_____

Listening and Speaking
Stick to the topic when speaking.
Tell about experiences in logical order.
Use descriptive words.
Report on topics using supportive details.

_____

_____

Language Conventions
Write in complete sentences.
Use end marks correctly.
Capitalize the first word in a sentence.
Capitalize names and I.
Use commas in the greeting and closing of a letter.
Use commas in dates.
Use commas for items in a series.

_____

_____

SOCIAL FOCUS FOR PROMPTS: Me / My Friends
My Neighborhood / My School

The Value of Reading
to Your Students Every Day

Reading is the key to becoming a lifelong learner. Reading introduces us to characters we will never meet, to places we will never visit, to situations we will never experience on our own. What a great way to introduce children to the wonders in their world! With our voices we bring entertainment and excitement. With the story, we bring visions and imagination. With our questions, we help students make connections to real life and give them opportunities to reflect and wonder. This is where writing ideas come from.

Read to your students every day. . .

- to entertain
- to motivate
- to model read aloud techniques
- to expose them to great literature
- to introduce them to a host of enjoyable characters
- to point out literary techniques they may use in their writing
- to expose them to varied types of illustrations
- to talk about artists' medium and technique
- to increase their knowledge base
- to show them how to make connections to their own lives
- to help them form opinions
- to encourage them to predict
- to paint imaginary visions in their heads
- to give them hope
- to allow them to dream
- to build their imaginations
- to help them formulate ideas for their own stories

Use daily read aloud time to introduce students to great writing techniques. Integrate writing mini lessons with that picture book read aloud. Start laying the foundation for writing skills and techniques that will make them successful. Start introducing them to The Simple 6™.

Teaching The Simple 6™ as You Read to Your Class

The actual implementation of The Simple 6™ writing program was initially intended for second semester of Grade 2. However, there are many short activities, as you read aloud to your students, that will introduce the common language, build a foundation, and make students aware of how the components of The Simple 6™ are found in any picture book. During or after a read aloud, teachers typically ask questions to engage students in thinking about the story. You may ask as few as three questions or as many as ten questions. Just consider replacing one of the questions you would ordinarily ask with *one* question or short activity from pages 13-15. Following is an overview of the basic ideas behind The Simple 6™. This will keep you focused as you integrate ideas for great writing with your picture book read aloud.

The Simple 6 ™

Quick Reference Guide for K-2 Students

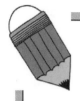

Stick to the Topic

- Stick to one idea. Don't ramble and repeat.
- Follow instructions.

Logical Order

- BME (Beginning, Middle, End)

Interesting Words

- Add at least 3 challenging words.

Varied Sentence Patterns

- Include questions, exclamations, and items in a series.
- Don't let your story sound like a list.

Descriptive Sentences

- Include many details.
- Appeal to the reader's senses.

Audience

- Let your personality shine! (exclamations, thoughts, and questions)

As You Read Aloud to Your Class . . .
15 Ideas
to help you integrate and make connections to

Stick to the Topic
1. Summarize the story in one sentence.
2. Discuss the main idea / details.

Logical Order
3. Choose 5 students to retell the story. BMMME
4. Walk through the pictures after reading.
5. Identify the strategy for the conclusion.

Interesting Words
6. Collect challenging vocabulary words from books.
7. Listen for precise *verbs*.

Varied Sentence Patterns
8. Practice question – answer.
9. Listen for exclamations.

Descriptive Sentences
10. Point out, reread, and discuss descriptive language.
11. Help students make connections to real life.
12. Have students illustrate a part of the story, but you MUST teach the drawing skills.
13. Focus on particular physical characteristics, especially in animals.

Audience
14. Point out books written in first person.
15. Read with expression.

Don't overdo it. Just choose one focus before you read.
On the next 2 pages are explanations of the 15 activities.

Stick to the Topic

1. Summarize the story in one sentence.
   Encourage students to give a story overview in one sentence. Two examples:
   This is the story of three pigs that go out into the world to seek their fortunes.
   This is the story of three pigs that leave their mother and build their own houses, but the wolf comes to blow the houses down!

2. Discuss the main idea/details.
   As you ask students to state the main idea of the story, help them to discover that the main idea and the topic are basically the same thing. Here, you are focusing only on introducing a new term to them.

Logical Order

3. Choose five students to retell the story.
   Turn them into HUMAN SENTENCES! Label five full-sized sheets of construction with B, M, M, M, E, and keep them face down until the end of the story. After reading, give them to five students who will line up in front of the room in order of Beginning, Middle, and End. Each student is allowed to tell one sentence for his part of the story. Focus on major events in the middles.

4. Walk through the pictures *after* reading.
   Have two chairs up front. This will give students a clue to the activity. At the end of the story, choose two students to take your place. One will hold the book, and the other will turn the pages. The two "teachers" will call on peers with raised hands to tell a sentence for each two-page spread.

5. Identify the strategy for the conclusion.
   Ask this simple question. What kind of ending does this story have?
   Choices: happy, sad, surprise, open, mystery solution, problem solution, others.

Interesting Words

6. Collect challenging vocabulary words from books.
   Put a full-sized sheet of construction paper on the board. Write the book title on top. Make a list with three stars. Have students identify interesting or challenging vocabulary words from the story. List them on the board. As a group, choose the best three. Write them on the chart. Use the words throughout the week. At the end of the week, put the chart at the student writing center for future use.

7. Listen for precise *verbs*.
   Talk about action words, especially those that might replace <u>went</u> and <u>said</u>.

Varied Sentence Patterns

8. Practice question – answer.
   Rather than asking students a question about the story, give the answer, and have students ask the question.

9. Listen for exclamations.
   Point them out and show them on the page. Possibly make a list of one-word exclamations for your Word Wall.

Descriptive Sentences

10. Point out, reread, and discuss descriptive language.

11. Help students make connections to real life.
    Ask students if the story reminds them of any real life experiences.

12. Have students illustrate a part of the story, but you MUST teach the drawing skills.
    Many times we provide students with materials and time to draw if they finish their other work. It is imperative that teachers take the time to teach students, step-by-step, what it takes to make an illustration.

13. Focus on particular physical characteristics of the characters, especially animals.
    How will you teach students to draw a person that looks real or a cow that looks like a cow and not a dog? Focus, break it down, and teach students to look at the world more critically. It takes practice and courage, but it is so worth it.

Audience

14. Point out books written in first person.
    Who is telling this story? Do we always know their names? Does it matter? Is there a stronger connection when you are reading a personal narrative?

15. Read with expression.
    There is no substitution for the teacher who comes to the read aloud with interest, drama, enthusiasm, and prior knowledge of the book.

The Read Aloud Recommendations

Following is an annotated list of read alouds that will help you focus on a single component of the Simple 6™. They are divided by component, but don't hesitate to use them for The Simple 6™ component of your choice. While these are suggestions for young students, you will find that any book you choose will have one or more Simple 6™ components upon which you can focus.

 ## STICK TO THE TOPIC

Books chosen for this Simple 6™ component have an easily identifiable topic or main idea. They may also have strengths in more than one other component.

TOPIC: DIFFERENCES
Painted Words/Spoken Memories, by Aliki (1998)
When Marian moves to America, she cannot understand the language. She records her memories in drawings until she can tell her stories in English. This is a great story that emphasizes the importance of art and drawing in communication.

TOPIC: FAMILY
Song and Dance Man, by Karen Ackerman (1988)
Grandpa takes the kids up to the attic and shows them what it was like in the good old days - when he was a song and dance man on the vaudeville stage.

The Memory Box, by Mary Bahr (1992)
Zach spends three weeks during the summer with his grandparents, working with them to create a memory box.

Just Like You, by Jan Fearnley (2000)
Mama Mouse and Little Mouse watch all the moms and dads getting their children ready for bed as they make their way back to their own home. This story has a great introduction for young writers, and the sequence is easy to follow.

Mama One, Mama Two, by Patricia MacLachlan (1982)
This heartwarming story tells about Maudie, who has gone into foster care until her mother recovers from depression.

Curious George, by H. A. Rey (1941)
This is the story of George the monkey and his adventures with his new family - the man in the large yellow straw hat. The simple sentence patterns are easy to read, but they would flow much better with more descriptions and better transitions. Kids don't seem to mind. They love Curious George!

The Relatives Came, by Cynthia Rylant (1985)
Once a year the relatives came from Virginia to visit. This ordinary family get-together that lasts for weeks tells about working, playing, eating, sleeping, and then returning to Virginia - until the same time next year.

TOPIC: GROWING UP
Verdi, by Janell Cannon (1997)
A baby python does not want to grow up and become slow and boring like the adults he observes. There are great synonyms in this book.

When I was Little, by Jamie Lee Curtis (1993)
This is the greatest book to inspire young writers to write their first autobiography. I love the compare-contrast element of the text, the age-appropriate comments, and the whimsical watercolor illustrations.

Oops-a-Daisy! by Claire Freedman (2004)
I like this book as motivation for young children who are learning to do something for the first time. As they grow up it gets easier, but they still need encouragement and practice, practice, practice.

When I am Eight, by Joan Lowery Nixon (1994)
A child with a vivid imagination describes what things will be like when he is eight like his brother. Told in first person, his comments are descriptive as well as entertaining.

TOPIC: LOVE
Koala Lou, by Mem Fox (1988)
Now that the family has grown, Koala Lou misses her mother saying, "Koala Lou, I DO love you!" She enters Bush Olympics to get attention. When she comes in second, she is disappointed, but Mother DOES say, "Koala Lou, I DO love you."

Guess How Much I Love You? by Sam McBratney (1994)
Little Nutbrown Hare and Big Nutbrown Hare make comparisons to all the things in the world as they tell how much they love one another. The repetitive nature of the text is great for young listeners.

The Giving Tree, by Shel Silverstein (1964)
In a moving story about a boy and a tree, we feel the tree's love for the boy. As the boy becomes a man, the tree gives him everything he has until there is nothing left but a stump. When the old man returns to sit on him, the tree is happy again. This book clearly illustrates giving without expecting anything in return.

YOUR FAVORITES. . .

LOGICAL ORDER

Expository or narrative, these books have a definite sense of order. Which have the best introductions and/or conclusions?

Bringing the Rain to Kapiti Plain, by Verna Aardema (1981)
This African tale, told in verse, is a cumulative story about the Kapiti Plain.

Up the Mountain, by Charlotte Agell (2000)
Four animal friends share their adventures from morning until night. This enjoyable story for young listeners is told in verse.

The Runaway Bunny, by Margaret Wise Brown (1972)
A little bunny is planning to run away from his mother. With each imaginative suggestion of how he will accomplish this, his mother finds an equally imaginative way to find him.

The Tiny Seed, by Eric Carle (1987)
This story follows the travels of a seed through the seasons. This easy-to-follow adventure has just the right amount of words on each page. Carle's descriptions and unique illustrations keep students engaged until the last page.

I am NOT Sleepy and I will NOT go to Bed, by Lauren Child (2001)
Charlie is in charge of getting Lola to bed, but as usual, she has a million other things on her mind. Step by step, we see all her methods of procrastination! Lola also makes a direct connection to the audience every time!

It Takes a Village, by Jane Cowen-Fletcher (1994)
This story is based on the African proverb, "It takes a village to raise a child." Its introduction is an excellent example of how young writers can develop a setting with just a few sentences at the beginning of their stories.

Terrible Teresa and Other Very Short Stories, by Mitti Cuetara (1997)
If you want short and to the point, this is the book for you! Each story is two pages long, divided into four pictures, and told with short, rhyming sentences. Can your students add a third middle?

Chicka Chicka Boom Boom, by Bill Martin, Jr. (1989)
As A tells B and B tells C all the letters move up the coconut tree. See what happens when they all get to the top! A great book for focusing on alphabetical order.

There's a Nightmare in my Closet, by Mercer Mayer (1968)
This book takes you step by step through the nightly rituals of a young boy as he makes sure there are no nightmares in his room.

Scritch Scratch, by Miriam Moss (2001)
This delightful book has all the Simple 6™ components, but its clear, logical order makes it easy for young students to see and understand how head lice spread. It also emphasizes the fact that anyone can get head lice - even the teacher!

The Cow that Went OINK, by Bernard Most (1990)
A cow that oinks and a pig that moos have the last laugh when they teach each other how to talk.

The Day Jimmy's Boa Ate the Wash, by Trinka Noble (1980)
This humorous book, illustrated by Steven Kellogg, tells the story of a (boring) class field trip - in reverse! This is a great example of cause and effect.

If you Give a Mouse a Cookie, by Laura Numeroff (1985)
If you give a mouse a cookie, he's going to want more and more and more and more, until finally - he's back to wanting a cookie. The text emphasizes logical order and has a repetitive nature that young listeners will love.

Night Sounds, Morning Colors, by Rosemary Wells (1994)
The story takes you step by step through the day. Examples of smooth transitions are excellent, but the author uses descriptive language, too.

Tuesday, by David Wiesner (1992)
This non-narrative story about the nightly adventures of frogs has outstanding illustrations. This book gives students an excellent opportunity to discuss, imagine, and create a wonderful story about a nocturnal adventure.

The Napping House, by Audrey Wood (1984)
A cumulative tale following the "House the Jack Built" pattern tells all about what happens when it's time to take a nap. Great for logical order but also for sentence patterns because of the repetition.

INTERESTING WORDS
(Challenging Vocabulary)

These authors use vocabulary to challenge young readers and listeners. While the words are usually known and meanings may be determined through context, generic vocabulary has been replaced by more interesting words.

Showdown at Slickrock, by Bagley, Pat (1995)
Bullfrog Ben raises havoc on the quiet town of Slickrock. This book has lots of challenging vocabulary and is written in verse to add to the fun!

The Mitten, by Jan Brett (1989)
This is a Ukranian tale about a boy named Nicki whose Baba makes him some mittens. Rich descriptions, realistic illustrations, and challenging vocabulary tell what happens when one of the mittens gets lost. A classic.

In the Small, Small Pond, by Denise Fleming (1993)
This author accomplishes so much with a book that has so little text. The illustrations are absolutely outstanding, and descriptions are rich but concise. While this book could also be used to focus on descriptive sentences and sentence patterns, The author presents a unique treatment of vocabulary.

Synonyms and Antonyms, by Ann Henrichs (2006)
Making a direct connection with its young audience, this book gives lots of examples, advice, and clear illustrations about the difference between synonyms and antonyms and how important they are in writing.

Chicken Little, retold by Steven Kellogg (1985)
This comical story is the retelling of the traditional fairy tale as only Steven Kellogg can. The story is filled with challenging vocabulary, but this humorous version is equally strong in connecting with the audience.

There's an Ant in Anthony, by Bernard Most (1980)
This quick read is just right for those students learning to find familiar word chunks in unknown words. Anthony finds the word *ant* everywhere! Great for beginning readers.

The Boy Who Cried Fabulous, by Leslea Newman (2004)
Roger's curiosity about all the fabulous wonders of the world always causes him to be late. When his parents ban him from using the word "fabulous," he is in a tizzy - until he gets to Marv's Diner!

Fancy Nancy, by Jane O'Connor (2006)
It will be hard to choose text over illustrations in this fun-filled book about being fancy. Nancy's adventures bring opportunities to learn many new, fancy words.

Tar Beach, by Faith Ringgold (1991)
This story reflects a young girl's thoughts and respect for the George Washington Bridge in New York City. Filled with imagination, interesting words, and descriptive ideas, this book takes you to the top floor of their apartment building - and tar beach.

Skippyjon Jones, by Judy Schachner (2003)
This book has examples of so many different kinds of words - in English and Spanish. You'll also find simple sentences, complex sentences, one-word exclamations, and examples of dialogue, song, and rhyme. This book is extremely entertaining!

Where the Wild Things Are, by Maurice Sendak (1963)
This wild tale of imaginary creatures is filled with descriptive illustrations and challenging vocabulary. One of young students' all time favorites, this book has the potential to inspire all kinds of interesting stories.

Doctor DeSoto, by William Steig (1982)
William Steig is always a first choice when it comes to books with challenging vocabulary. In this story, Dr. DeSoto, the mouse dentist, outsmarts the devious fox so he and his wife aren't eaten. It also has the surprise ending!

Amazing Snakes! by Sarah L. Thomson (2006)
This I Can Read book teaches students new words such as prey, constrictors, venom, survive, and hibernate as they learn about snakes.

Two Bad Ants, by Chris Van Allsburg (1988)
This is a very descriptive tale of two ants that stay behind (in the sugar bowl) and have all kinds of exciting adventures. They are relieved when their ant friends finally return for more crystals. They go to the back of the line and return home - where they belong. Great vocabulary.

YOUR FAVORITES. . .

DIFFERENT SENTENCE PATTERNS

Books that have questions, exclamations, and noticeable patterns help young students learn to eliminate list-like writing.

Miss Nelson is Missing, by Harry Allard (1977)
The students in Room 207 misbehave so badly that their teacher comes back as a witch! Sentence patterns are relatively short and easy to read, but the effect of narration and dialogue make the words flow.

Who Sank the Boat? by Pamela Allen (1988)
There are lots of questions and answers in this quick read about a mouse that sank a boat!

I Ain't Gonna Paint No More! by Karen Beaumont (2005)
To the tune of "It Ain't Gonna Rain," this little boy just can't stop painting! The book is filled with repetition, verse, and imaginative, colorful pictures.

The Pain and The Great One, by Judy Blume (1974)
Written as free verse, the two stories in this book express the frustrations a sister has over her younger brother and her older sister.

Where do Balloons Go?, by Jamie Lee Curtis (2000)
What a great book to emphasize the importance of asking questions as you write! Written in verse, this colorfully illustrated book poses many questions about what happens when your balloon gets away from you.

Warthogs Paint: A Messy Color Book, by Pamela Edwards (2001)
It's a rainy day, so the warthogs decide to stay in and paint. The author's use of onomato-poeia, color words, sentence patterns, and verse make it an entertaining choice.

Guess What? by Mem Fox (1988)
Questions guide young readers through this story about a not-so-mean witch.

Is Your Mama a Llama? by Deborah Guarino (1989)
With a combination of questions and answers, as well as text that rhymes, this book gives great examples for those students focusing on different sentence patterns.

Mama Don't Allow, by Thacher Hurd (1984)
This comical story is filled with questions, exclamations, dialogue, and repetition. Students will love the surprise ending!

Leo the Late Bloomer, by Robert Kraus (1971)
Leo wasn't developing as soon as his father thought he should. Finally, he can do many things, but he does it in his own time. The text has an effective use of short sentences, repetition, and conversation.

A Quilt for Baby, by Kim Lewis (2002)
With a gentle voice, a young mother talks to her baby about where they live. Descriptive statements, questions, and conversation with the baby will lull you to sleep.

Brown Bear, Brown Bear, What Do You See? by Bill Martin (1967, 1995)
Young students see a brown bear, a yellow duck, a blue horse, and other animals as they alternate between questions and answers throughout the book.

Suddenly! by Colin McHaughton (1994)
Help your students get rid of the "and then-itis" with this fun book about a pig who is being followed by a wolf!

Punctuation Takes a Vacation, by Robin Pulver (2003)
Mr. Wright's students go crazy when all their punctuation takes a vacation. This book has excellent examples of varied sentence patterns and use of punctuation.

Fortunately by Charlie Remy (1964, 1993)
Ned's luck goes from bad to good and back again many times over as he tries to get to a surprise party. Fortunately, this book has unique style. Unfortunately, all the sentence patterns are very similar.

Crocodile Listens, by April Sayre (2001)
Despite the short sentences and repetitive nature, this book has a style all its own. Onomatopoeia leads the way on almost every page as a crocodile egg hatches.

No, David! by David Shannon (1998)
This quickie is filled with exclamations as David gets into one thing after another. At the end of the day, things calm down - when he finally falls asleep.

YOUR FAVORITES. . .

DESCRIPTIVE SENTENCES

Look for the strategies for writing sentences that are more descriptive: precise verbs, proper nouns, adjectives, imagery, and other literary devices such as simile or metaphor. Using your most expressive voice, take the extra minute to stop and reread. (Don't forget the importance of modeling these strategies with the use of non-narrative books!)

Journey of the Nightly Jaguar, by Albert Burton (1996)
Artistic and descriptive pages fill the reader with visions of an endangered species - the jaguar.

Turtle in the Sea, by Jim Arnosky (2002)
This quick read aloud has wonderfully descriptive language for young students.

When Sophie Gets Angry — Really, Really Angry. . . by Molly Bang (1999)
Vibrant colors and vivid metaphors tell this short story of a temper tantrum.

Things that are MOST in the World, by Judi Barrett (2001)
This quick-read book of superlatives has outstanding comparisons and realistic pictures.

Noisy Breakfast, by Ellen Blonder (1994)
This quick-read has many short sentences that appeal to the sense of hearing. As a mouse and a dog have breakfast, you'll hear the sounds as precise verbs. This VERY short text would be used as an introduction to precise verbs for beginning writers.

The Important Book, by Margaret Wise Brown (1949, 1977)
From spoon to sky, from apples to rain - you'll learn what's important in this unique book that appeals to the reader's senses.

My Mom, by Anthony Browne (2005)
Filled with adjectives and similes, this quick read helps young writers think beyond descriptors like *nice*.

Frank and Ernest, by Alexandra Day (1991)
Frank and Ernest take care of Mrs. Miller's diner while she is away, and they learn that there is a whole new language in the restaurant business.

Fidgety Fish, by Ruth Galloway (2001)
Tiddler, the fidgety fish, has an exciting adventure when his mom sends him out to get rid of some of his energy. Great examples of precise verbs!

One Dark Night, by Hazel Hutchins (2001)
There is plenty of simile and metaphor in this descriptive book about a stormy night. Short text.

The Antic Alphabet, by Lena Lencek (1994)
This unusual alphabet book helps students create a two-part visual image from one word.

Listen to the Rain, by Bill Martin and John Archambault (1988)
Rhythmic, descriptive sentences paint a perfect picture of the sounds and silences of rain. Short text.

With a Dog Like That, a Kid Like Me . . . by Michael J. Rosen (2000)
This quick read gives a new example of metaphor and precise verbs on every page!

Hello Ocean, by Pam Munoz Ryan (2001)
There are so many examples of descriptive language in this short book about a day at the beach. Onomatopoeia, personification, metaphor, and imagery emerge from these lines of verse.

Old Mac Donald had a Woodshop, by Lisa Schulman (2002)
In this quick read, students hear the sounds of each tool as Old MacDonald builds a farm in HER workshop.

Rain Talk, by Mary Serfozo (1990)
The book has relatively simple sentence patterns but gives great examples of onomatopoeia and metaphor as it begins to rain.

Car Wash, by Sandra and Susan Steen (2001)
Descriptive language, metaphor, short clippie sentences, and one-word ideas give this book a very unique style!

Vincent's Colors, by Vincent Van Gogh (2005)
In Vincent's own words, he simply describes some of the details in his paintings.

YOUR FAVORITES. . .

AUDIENCE/VOICE

There is a special tone or style in these books that totally engages young students. The authors bring their personalities to the reader/listener using various types of engaging techniques.

I Will Never Not Ever Eat a Tomato, by Lauren Child (2000)
Lola is a very fussy eater. Charlie connects with the audience as he tells how he gets his sister to eat, but his technique is SO effective because of the way he describes each food item.

Click, Clack, Moo Cows that Type, by Doreen Cronin (2000)
The author makes a direct connection to the reader as the cows go on strike to get better conditions in the barn. Hilarious!

Diary of a Worm, by Doreen Cronin (2003)
This diary, written by a young worm, focuses on the advantages and disadvantages of being a worm as well as thoughts on behavior, adventure, and life lessons.

Please Say Please! Penguin's Guide to Manners, by Margery Cuyler (2004)
This is a great book to introduce manners to young children. It has just the right amount of questions, personal comments, and exclamations to connect the reader and writer! You could, however, also use this book to show different types of sentence patterns.

How to Get a Gorilla Out of Your Bathtub, by John Hall (2006)
A very precocious little girl will tell you exactly how to get a gorilla out of your bathtub! She explains several ideas you would not want to try before she finally lets you know that all you need to say is, "Please!" This one is great for logical order as well.

Achoo! Bang! Crash! The Noisy Alphabet, by Ross Macdonald (2003)
Lots of one-word descriptors and exclamations to connect with the audience.

Mrs. Watson Wants Your Teeth, by Alison McGhee (2004)
This story is LOADED with thought shots that make the reader feel the apprehension of going to a new class. . .with a new (alien) teacher. . .who needs baby teeth to survive! There are also some obvious transitions that help students identify events.

I Stink! by Kate and Jim McMullan (2002)
Who stinks? The garbage truck, that's who! This book tells all about garbage pickups - while you sleep!

Cow, by Jules Older (1997)
This book is full of examples of connecting with the audience! Older writes in a style that makes voice just pop out of the pages for students and teachers alike! Logical order is a strong second choice here!

Pig, by Jules Older (2004)
I LOVE this author's style. His books so clearly give students (and teachers) examples of connecting directly with the audience. As you read this comical, informative book about pigs to your class, I dare you not to smile!

Psssst! It's Me. . .The Bogeyman, by Barbara Park (1998)
Written in first person, this book not only has GREAT voice but also gives wonderful examples of descriptive sentences.

My Rotten Redheaded Older Brother, by Patricia Polacco (1994)
The author tells a story from her childhood and makes a direct connection with the reader as she describes the frustration of being a younger sister who isn't the best at anything.

Alexander, Who's Not (Do you hear me? I mean it!) Going to Move, by J. Viorst (1991)
Combining short and long sentences - and even some fragments - Alexander makes his point. He does NOT like the idea that his family is moving!

Alexander, Who Used to Be Rich Last Sunday, by Judith Viorst (1978) All the Alexander books are entertaining, and this one is certainly no exception. You know EXACTLY how Alexander feels every step of the way. His comments are funny, frank, and straight from the heart. Find out how Alexander used to be rich, but now all he has is . . . bus tokens.

The Three Pigs, by David Wiesner (2001)
This is quite a unique version of the tale of the three pigs. Wiesner combines the traditional story with additional pigs that have been inserted on each page, offering humorous commentary along the way.

Don't Let the Pigeon Drive the Bus! by Mo Willems (2003)
The pictures and text in this quick read are so SIMPLE that young children love this character! Pigeon's comments give a very clear idea of connecting with the audience as he tells about why he should be able to drive the bus!

YOUR FAVORITES. . .

Your Top 10 Picture Book Choices
For Read Alouds

BOOK TITLE	AUTHOR	SIMPLE 6™ REINFORCEMENT

SUGGESTION: Instead of reading five books a week to your class, read four. Read the Monday, Tuesday, and Wednesday books just for fun and discussion. The Thursday book will become the "Masterpiece Book," and you will spend two days on it.

Use the following pages to help organize your lesson plans as you reinforce The Simple 6™ component, teach the drawing skills, design an art project, and integrate a writing connection. Collaborate and share with colleagues by keeping the lesson plans in a binder or attaching them in the back of each picture book.

Getting the Most out of a Picture Book

Title/Author _____ Location _____

SUMMARY_____
_____
_____

KEY ILLUSTRATIONS / ART INTEGRATION
_____
_____
_____

WRITING CONNECTION
_____
_____
_____

Stick to the Topic:
List related story ideas. Make connections.
Brainstorm by modeling a web.
Retell the story using a graphic organizer such as a story map.

Logical Order:
Introduce BMMME. Create human sentences.
Arrange paper story strips in sequential order.
Engage students in a picture walk-through.
Discuss introduction and/or conclusion strategies.

Interesting Words:
Discuss and question as you read.
Create a Word Wall.
List special words.

Varied Sentence Patterns:
Listen for questions and exclamations.

Descriptive Sentences:
Point out descriptive language.

Audience:
Have students identify who is telling the story.
Listen for sentences that connect the writer with the audience.

Getting the Most out of a Picture Book

Title/Author _____ Location _____

SUMMARY_____

_____

_____

KEY ILLUSTRATIONS / ART INTEGRATION

_____

_____

_____

WRITING
CONNECTION_____

_____

_____

Stick to the Topic:

Logical Order:

Interesting Words:

Varied Sentence Patterns:

Descriptive Sentences:

Audience:

Chapter 2:   Teaching Young Students to Draw

Books for Motivating Students to be Artists

Drawing Picture Book Characters with Young Writers

> Pigeon
> Maisy
> Arthur
> Lyle
> Spot
> Chrysanthemum (Lilly)
> Clifford
> Other Favorites

Chapter 2: Teaching Young Students to Draw

My classroom was always buzzing with integrated, creative activities, but one that my students thoroughly enjoyed took place every Thursday and carried over into Friday. It was the creation of "The Masterpiece." By choosing four books to read aloud each week rather than five, I could spend two days on my Thursday choice – brainstorming, planning, drawing, and writing to create a Masterpiece!

In order to be successful, you need to believe you can draw better than your students can. You need to be able to see pictures and illustrations broken down into teachable parts, you need to be willing to take the time to draw, color, and paint, and you need to be enthusiastic and encouraging. Below are books you might read to students early in the year that will set the stage for all the fun they are going to have in your class!

Books for Motivating Students to be Artists

To Be an Artist, by Maya Ajmera and John Ivanko (2004)
Being an artist means more than just drawing and painting. It means being a dancer, a performer, a musician, a sculptor, or a writer. Student artists from almost 40 countries are featured in vibrant photographs.

Willy's Pictures, by Anthony Browne (2000)
Willy puts a twist on famous paintings when he exchanges real subjects for chimps. He adds a caption and instantly has an idea for an imaginary story! This book will motivate students to examine, analyze, integrate, and create pictures as well as stories.

Emily's Art, by Peter Catalanotto (2001)
First graders learn the difference between a contest and a race and how judging can be influenced by personal experiences. Students learn about fairness, disappointment, and painting from the heart. While the characters in this book are primary students, this book has valuable lessons for all ages about what is *best*.

The Art Lesson, by Tomie dePaola (1989)
Tommy knows from the time he is very young that he wants to be an artist. He practices drawing and coloring and can't wait to start school where he will have a real art teacher. When the art teacher wants him to copy what she does, they compromise - and the rest is history!

Begin at the Beginning: A Little Artist Learns about Life, by Amy Schwartz (1983)
Sara's teacher has chosen her to paint a wonderful painting for the second grade art show. Sara struggles with getting started until she realizes that she should start small – with the tree outside her bedroom window. This is a great connection for students who have trouble zeroing in on a single topic.

Drawing Picture Book Characters with Young Writers

When was the last time you stood at the board with chalk or marker in hand and drew something step by step with your students? It is necessary, you know. While many teachers don't have the courage to try, it is really very easy if you practice. Where will you get the ideas for the characters you will draw? The most logical place to start is with the picture books you read each week!

As you consider the possibility . . .

Step 1.   Look for characters that can be drawn with recognizable shapes, letters, and numbers. There are suggestions on the following pages.

Step 2.   Avoid drawing characters from the ¾ view. Head on is best, but there are some drawn from a side view. Keep it simple.

Step 3.   Practice at home with blank paper or a sketchbook.

REMEMBER: It's not always about drawing the character! Being able to draw the main character, however, is a very strong motivator for getting kids to read more. Many books have amazing art projects in them that do not include the main character. You just have to look! And don't worry . . . as you do more art projects with students that are based on picture book reading, they will find the project for you!

As you prepare students for the big event . . .

Step 1.   Establish the "rules" first.
* Watch and listen.
* Draw immediately after I tell you to.
* Erase as little as possible.
* Stay with me.
* If you run into a problem, raise your hand for help.
* Sketch, don't gouge. (Practice first with lines and simple shapes.)
* Concentrate. Don't talk to your neighbors.

Step 2.   Make sure desks are totally cleared off and everyone is facing the board. Move desks around if necessary.

Step 3.   Give paper and pencils to all students. Erasers are optional. You might have an art eraser for each student that is only used during drawing lessons.

As you approach the board for your first drawing lesson . . .

You CAN do this. You have practiced the night before, and you have the step-by-step directions or your completed drawing in your hand. Remember, it is more about motivation than about anything else. If students can draw a storybook character, they want to listen to or read more stories about that character. The more they know about that character, the more interested they will be in writing about him. Take students through the lesson one step at a time. Be patient. Your students will need time to adjust to this new skill. They will listen, follow instructions, and go faster as time goes on.

Step 1.   Don't start the lesson by saying, "Now kids, I'm not an artist. . ." You CAN draw better than your students can. Just do it.

Step 2.   Draw the outline of the paper on the board so students can see their workspace. Leave room to the left so you can list descriptive words you use as you draw.

Step 3.   Help students plan their space by folding the paper and using their hands to create guidelines and "margins" to draw to or within.

Step 4.   Start with a basic shape. Use students' hands and fingers to make guidelines for the size of the main object.

Step 5.   Guide them through, step by step. Show them what you will draw, draw it on the board as they watch, and then instruct them to draw on their papers.

Step 6.   After a minute or so, go to the next part.

Step 7.   Occasionally, walk around the room, making sure everyone is keeping up. Get help from parents who are artistic. Just make sure that they don't draw on students' papers! Have small pieces of paper ready for close-up demonstrations, or bring individuals to the board.

Step 8. Complete the pencil drawing in one sitting – usually 30 minutes, depending on grade level. This will be hard at first, so start with something VERY SIMPLE.
Establish this pattern for students.
You explain - they listen.
You demonstrate - they watch.
You wait - they draw.

Step 9. Finish the main object. Start the background, using the same procedures. Allow students to get out of their seats and look out the window. Help them to see that their environment is more than a "green strip" ground and a "blue strip" sky.

Step 10. Save the coloring for the next day.

Speaking of coloring, teach your students how to color early in the year. Show them how to blend, not scribble. Point out that if their hands stay on the page and only their fingers move, there will be fewer white spots to fill in later. Take the time to demonstrate this! Work with students one-on-one if necessary. These few minutes can carry over for a lifetime!

Suggested Time Schedule:

Thursday

9:00 – 9:15   Read the story. Make the Simple 6™ connection.
9:15 -- 9:45 Draw the picture.
9:45 – 10:00 Discuss possible writing activities or introduce the writing activity and start writing.

Friday

9:00 – 9:10   Review the writing activity.
9:10 – 9:40   Write. (You will be circulating and helping individuals.)
9:40 –10:00   Recopy final draft, continue getting help, or color the picture. If the whole hour is needed for writing, color the picture later in the day as a separate activity.

As students start writing more, especially in Grade 2, you may want to focus on writing the entire rough draft Thursday morning. Schedule a 30- 45-minute art time on Thursday afternoon, when you will take them step by step through the drawing. List potential descriptive words on the board. Discuss background and details. Start writing revisions the next morning. Having the drawing lesson in between makes a huge impact!

Following are easy characters and art projects to get you started. They are arranged in order of difficulty. Copyright issues prevent giving the complete step-by-step directions, but the basic shape is presented with additional guidelines and a completed student sample. Use the pictures in your read aloud to get the rest of the information you need.

Integrated Activities for Picture Books
MO WILLEMS

PART 1   THE READ ALOUD: *Don't Let the Pigeon Drive the Bus!* (2003)

Summary: When the bus driver takes a break, he leaves these instructions: "Don't let the pigeon drive the bus!" The pigeon does his best to be persuasive, but soon the bus driver returns and takes off. Suddenly a truck approaches. . .

The **Simple 6** ™ FOCUS: Audience

The author makes a direct appeal to the reader to help out.

PART II: THE DRAWING
    Draw the pigeon.

This is the easiest character
on the market, which is why
it is in the number 1 slot.

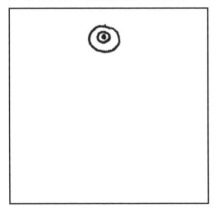

Start with the circle for the head.
Draw two more circles for the eye.
Add a rectangle for the neck.
Add the horizontal line by making a
stretched out L.
Turn the paper sideways and make
a C for the body.
Add two legs. (number 1)
Add feet. (upside down V)
Draw beak. (sideways V)
Add neck stripe and wing.

PART III: THE ART PROJECT IDEA

The beauty of any project here is the mere simplicity of it. Using simple shapes cut from construction paper, make the bus, the truck, or any other vehicle. Pigeon's head can be drawn in the window. OR Cut out a window in the front. Make pigeon from construction paper shapes (head only), and glue him into his place behind the wheel!

PART IV: THE WRITING CONNECTION

Why Can't the Pigeon Drive the Bus?
Don't let the Pigeon Drive. . .

      the boat
      the new car
      the tractor
      the police car
      the fire truck

Don't let the Pigeon Fly the Plane
Don't let the Pigeon. . .

If I were a Pigeon
The Day I Drove a Bus

also by Mo Willems . . .

PART 1   THE READ ALOUD: *Don't Let the Pigeon Stay Up Late* (2006)

Summary: While the man brushes his teeth, he appeals to the reader to not let the pigeon stay up. After many excuses and pleas, the pigeon just can't keep his eyes open any longer.

 **FOCUS: Different Sentence Patterns**

Lots of statements, questions, and exclamations give students clear examples.

PART II: ART PROJECT IDEA

Draw the pigeon with his eye closed instead of open.
Using graph paper, make a quilt and cover the pigeon.

PART III: THE WRITING CONNECTION

My Bedtime Routine
The Time I Stayed Up Late
My Favorite Stuffed Animal
Why I Like to Stay Up

Other Pigeon books . . .

      The Pigeon Finds a Hot Dog (2004)
      The Pigeon Has Feelings Too! (2005)
      The Pigeon Loves Things that Go! (2005)

Integrated Activities for Picture Books
LUCY COUSINS

PART 1   **THE READ ALOUD:** *Maisy Makes Gingerbread* (1999)

Summary: Step by step, Maisy makes gingerbread cookies.

The Simple 6 ™   **FOCUS: Logical Order**

PART II: **THE DRAWING**
                 Draw Maisy.

Start with a sideways V.
Stretch it out.
Draw a circle where the 2 lines
come together.

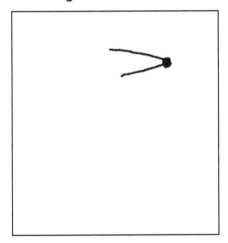

Add 2 circles for ears.
Fill in 2 small circles for eyes.
Make a small V for the mouth.
Finish the neck with a straight line.
Add more straight lines for whiskers.
Draw the body.

PART III: THE ART PROJECT IDEA

Make a poster. Give the step-by-step instructions for something you know how to make.
At the top, write Maisy Makes _____. Draw Maisy on the left side of your
poster. Make her hand point to your directions. List your directions one by one. Don't forget to number them!

PART IV: THE WRITING CONNECTION

Sharing with Your Friends   Maisy Makes _____
The Day I Made Gingerbread Cookies   Cooking is Fun!
Maisy Loses the Recipe

also by Lucy Cousins . . .

PART 1   THE READ ALOUD: *Maisy Goes Camping* (2004)
Summary: On Maisy's camping trip everyone helps to pitch the tent. When they all try to get in to sleep, it's too crowded. One by one, they pop out to sleep under the stars.

The Simple 6 ™ FOCUS: Sentence Patterns
                    Also: Logical Order (transition words)

Even though this story is told in simple sentence patterns, there are several different types. Beginning with a complex sentence and ending with an exclamation, this book has examples of sentence patterns for beginning writers. Also: Great use of transitions squeezing into the tent and repetition popping out of the tent.

PART II: ART PROJECT IDEA

The characters in the story are seen as silhouettes once they are inside the tent. Draw the characters with white chalk on black construction paper, cut them out, and put them "in" the tent. OR
Make two large murals of the woods. Put a large tent in each scene. Half of the students could put black silhouettes inside their tents, and the other half could make colored characters outside their tents. Glue characters onto the scene. Use marker or paint to put the details into the camping area.

PART III: THE WRITING CONNECTION

Maisy's Great Idea   The Best Camping Trip Ever   My Camping Song
Room for One More   Working Together   Fun with Friends
The Wise Old Owl   Maisy Goes _____

Other Maisy books . . .
Maisy Dresses Up, (1999)   *How will you get There, Maisy? (2004)*
Maisy Drives the Bus, (2000)   *Maisy Goes to the Library, (2005)*
Maisy at the Fair, (2001)   *Maisy, Charley, and the Wobbly Tooth, (2006)*
Where are you Going, Maisy? (2003)

Integrated Activities for Picture Books
MARC BROWN

PART 1   **THE READ ALOUD:** *Arthur's Family Vacation* (1993)

Summary: Arthur's family takes a vacation during camp week! The hotel is terrible. Then it rains. Arthur saves the day by creating indoor field trips and the vacation is saved!

The Simple 6 ™   **FOCUS: Different Sentence Patterns**

As you read the picture book to your class, focus on the different sentence patterns. As the story is narrated, the sentences are statements. As the characters talk to one another, they use questions and exclamations. Have students give you a signal when they hear a question or an exclamation.

PART II: THE DRAWING
Draw Arthur.

Start with an upside down U.
Add 2 circles for his glasses.

Add a half circle below the glasses.
Draw a smile.
Add 2 beady eyes.
Make 2 upside-down U's for nostrils.
Add eyebrows.
Make his ears.

PART III: THE ART PROJECT IDEA
Summer Fun with Arthur
Make a bulletin board using the picture on the title page. Draw Arthur's head, cut it out, put the head (with or without arms) inside the inner tube. Use butcher paper and yarn to create the water. Add writing if desired.

Using teacher-made body patterns make a life-sized Arthur. Be sure to bend one arm so Arthur can hold up the writing for display. Let students design and color the clothing and the head. Bend one arm, and put the writing in it for display.

PART IV: THE WRITING CONNECTION

Write a letter to Marc Brown about the book.
Write a postcard to a friend.
Write a new story about Arthur.

Write a letter to Arthur about your vacation.

also by Marc Brown . . .

PART 1   THE READ ALOUD: *Arthur's Teacher Trouble* (1986)
Summary: Arthur gets Mr. Ratburn as his teacher. While every other class in the school is easing into their routine, Arthur has homework every night. As he studies day and night for the school-wide Spellathon, DW reminds him that she has plenty of time to play. She doesn't have homework because she won't be in kindergarten until next year – and Ms. Meeker never gives homework. After Arthur wins the Spellathon, Mr. Ratburn makes an announcement. Next year he'll be teaching kindergarten!

 **FOCUS: Logical Order**

I like the way the story progresses with a task, hard work, and a reward when Arthur wins the Spellathon. The best part, though, is the surprise ending!

PART II: ART PROJECT IDEA

Make a notebook-sized template for a page in a Writer's Notebook. At the top, label it TOUGHEST WORDS FOR GRADE ___. Draw Arthur's face in the upper left hand corner. As a class, decide on the toughest 20 spelling words. Type them in an alphabetized list. Leave room at the bottom for each student to add their own words. Students will place the sheets in their Writer's Notebooks for quick reference.

PART III: THE WRITING CONNECTION

The Spelling Bee
My Teacher is the (Best or Worst)!
I Really Felt Proud When. . .
My Teacher, Mr. Ratburn

How I REALLY Feel about Homework
Hard Work Always Pays
DW's First Day of Kindergarten

Other Arthur books . . .
Arthur's Birthday (1989)
Arthur's Underwear (2001)
The World of Arthur and Friends (2004)

Arthur Goes to Camp (1982)
Arthur's Computer Disaster (1997)
Arthur's Off to School (2004)
Arthur Helps Out (2005)

Integrated Activities for Picture Books
BERNARD WABER

PART 1   **THE READ ALOUD:** *Lyle, Lyle, Crocodile* (1965)

Summary: Lyle loves his house on 88th Street, but his neighbor Mr. Grumps doesn't appreciate Lyle and his antics. One day he goes shopping with his owner Mrs. Primm, and he ends up performing an old vaudeville act in the pajama department with his old partner, Signor Valenti. Mr. Grumps gets him sent to the zoo, where he is miserable. Signor Valenti helps him escape, just in time to save Mr. Grumps and his cat Loretta from the burning building. All is well at the end.

The Simple 6 ™   **FOCUS: Sentence Patterns**
                                              Interesting Words

Different sentence patterns is my first choice, because they are effective but not overwhelming. Vocabulary is excellent, with many challenging words as well as precise verbs.

PART II: **THE DRAWING**
                  Draw Lyle.

Start with a capital U that
faces the corner.

Make his forehead look like the
top of a heart.
Extend a second line down the side of his jaw.
Add nostrils.
Add eyes and eyebrows.

PART III: THE ART PROJECT

For starters, you can always draw Lyle in the bathtub. That eliminates the bottom half of his body. I also like the picture of Lyle helping Joshua with his math facts. The best side views are on the page with Signor Valenti in the department store, with Signor Valenti in the jail, and the final page with Loretta.

PART IV: THE WRITING CONNECTION

Lyle Goes Shopping	Lyle Meets an Old Friend	Lyle Saves the Day
Lyle, My Hero	Our Friend Lyle	
A Crocodile in the Neighborhood	Old Mr. Grumps or New Mr. Grumps?	

Also by Bernard Waber . . .

PART 1   THE READ ALOUD: *Lyle Finds his Mother* (1974)

Summary: Signor Valenti is down on his luck so he sends a letter to Lyle asking if Lyle would like to see his mother. He figures Lyle will come, and they will return to their Vaudeville act. After many performances, Signor finally takes Lyle to an obscure swamp far away. As luck would have it, Lyle's mother is there. She returns with Lyle to the house on 88th St.

The **Simple6** ™ FOCUS: **Logical Order**
                                                         Interesting Words

There are easily identifiable major events in this story, as well as the happy ending. Waber also adds challenging vocabulary.

PART II: THE ART PROJECT

It will be easy to draw a family portrait of Lyle and his mother. All you have to do is draw two Lyles, and add a hat and a locket to one of them. Be sure to make a frame out of construction paper and glue it on.

PART III: THE WRITING CONNECTION

The Day I Turned into a Crocodile	My Mother
Happy at Last!	Back on the Stage
If I Lived in the Swamp	

Other Lyle books . . .

The House on East 88th Street (1973)	*Lyle and the Birthday Party (1973)*
Lovable Lyle (1977)	*Funny, Funny Lyle (1991)*
Lyle at the Office (1996)	*Lyle at Christmas (2003)*

Integrated Activities for Picture Books
ERIC HILL

PART 1   THE READ ALOUD: *Where's Spot?* (1980)

Summary: Spot is missing, and it's time for dinner! Where can Spot be?

The Simple 6 ™   **FOCUS: Varied Sentence Patterns**

Use this quick read to focus on questions for beginning writers.

PART II: **THE DRAWING**
              Draw Spot.

While Spot has simple lines, he is not as easy to draw as the other characters we have practiced.

Start with a Capital C.
Take away the roundness at the bottom.
Add a capital U.

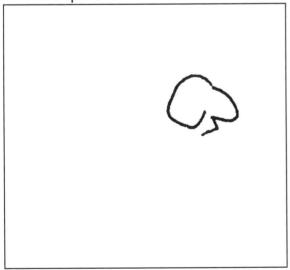

Underneath, make a sideways V.
Make a horizontal line that slopes up at the left.
Make a curved vertical line.
Add a short horizontal line for the body.
Add rectangles for the legs.
Add dots for eyes, nose, and whiskers.
Add commas for paws.

PART III: ART PROJECT IDEA

What an opportunity to make a flap book with Spot inside! Check out the simple pictures of Sally throughout this book and use them to draw Spot. He only needs to be smaller if Sally is in the picture, too! Start with the great side view on the first page of the story.
Ask the question at the top: Where's Spot?
Answer the question at the bottom: He's in the closet!
(Use the idea from the book or an original idea.)

PART IV: THE WRITING CONNECTION

The Day Spot Got Lost	The Day I Got Lost	Where's Spot?
Who is Spot?	My Favorite Hiding Place	Hide-and-Go-Seek

also by Eric Hill . . .

PART 1   THE READ ALOUD: _My First Walk_ (1981)

Summary: Spot's friends watch out for him as he ventures out for his first walk by himself. Peek behind the flaps to see what he learns!

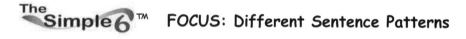 **FOCUS: Different Sentence Patterns**

This story is told in simple sentences, using exclamations, questions, and pictures.

PART II: ART PROJECT IDEA

This is a great book to teach students to see simple backgrounds. Draw Spot. Then place him in the various places he visited. Help students choose one, and draw it step by step. Point out that there are no "green strips" for ground and "blue strips" for sky.

PART III: THE WRITING CONNECTION

All By Myself
What Are You Doing?
My First Walk
Today I Saw. . .
My Fun Day
Don't Go Too Far

Other Spot books . . .	_Spot's Birthday Party (1982)_
Spot Goes to the Beach (2003)	_Spot Bakes a Cake (1994)_
Spot Visits his Grandparents (1995)	_Spot Goes to the Farm (2003)_

Integrated Activities for Picture Books
KEVIN HENKES

PART 1   **THE READ ALOUD:** *Chrysanthemum* (1996)

Summary: Chrysanthemum LOVES her name until she gets to school and the other students start making fun of it. Her teacher saves the day when she names her new baby Chrysanthemum.

The Simple 6 ™   **FOCUS: Different Sentence Patterns**

Henkes writes with short, effective sentence patterns that are just right for this age level. His use of a repetitive pattern keeps students engaged and entertained.

PART II: **THE DRAWING**
                Draw Chrysanthemum.

Start with a sideways teardrop.
Add a capital C.
Draw a smaller capital C inside it.

Draw a stretched out U for the eyes and mouth.
Draw a flared triangle for the dress.
Add arms with thumbs toward the body.
Draw the legs.
Add shoes that look like stretched out Cs.

PART III: ART PROJECT IDEA

The most inspiring picture of Chrysanthemum shows her skipping off to school. I would use this picture to show students that a tissue can be used as an eraser when you are painting! Tape student-grade watercolor paper to each desk. Have students paint the paper with water, dropping in some blue color (for a wet on wet wash for the sky). Draw Chrysanthemum on a small, white, construction-paper cloud. Glue the cloud onto the painting of the sky. Add details with marker or crayon, or cut out flowers and leaves from construction paper, and glue them on for a total three-dimensional look.

PART IV: THE WRITING CONNECTION

How I Got My Name
If I Could Have Any Name
The Best Name in the World

also by Kevin Henkes . . .

PART I: THE READ ALOUD: *Lilly's Purple Plastic Purse* (1996)

Summary: Mr. Slinger is not amused when Lilly brings a purple purse to school that makes noise and bothers the other students. He takes her purse until the end of the day, and she draws him a mean picture. Mr. Slinger writes her a nice note and gives her some special snacks when he returns the purse. She feels much better after she writes a story about how nice and forgiving he is.

The Simple 6 ™ FOCUS: Descriptive Sentences

I like the way this story is told. It focuses on feelings and lessons about behavior. The language is effective as well as entertaining.

Part II: THE DRAWING
Draw Lilly
(Follow the directions for Chrysanthemum — just add boots!)

On the very first page of the story, there is a side view of Lilly that is easy to draw. Focus on the tear drop-shaped head, the triangular-shaped dress, arms straight out to the sides, with one leg vertical and the other horizontal to show that she is running. Another simple drawing shows Lilly raising her hand to be called on throughout the day. A third, full-body example shows sad Lilly after her purse was taken.

PART III: THE ART PROJECT
When I Grow Up. . .

The last page in the story talks about Lilly wanting to be a teacher – on the days she doesn't want to be a doctor, dancer, or scuba diver. Draw Lilly as the character you would like to be when you grow up.

PART IV: THE WRITING CONNECTION
Write a letter to Mr. Slinger apologizing for the picture. Sign it *Lilly.*
What I Want to Be When I Grow Up
Tomorrow is a Better Day
I am So So So So Sorry
_____ is So Nice! (Glue the story to a purple purse frame!)

other Lilly books . . .   *A Box of Treats: Five Little Picture Books
                                     about Lilly and Her Friends (2004)
                                   Lilly's Big Day (2006)*

Integrated Activities for Picture Books
NORMAN BRIDWELL

PART 1   **THE READ ALOUD:** *Clifford, the Big Red Dog* (1985)

Summary: Emily Elizabeth has a big red dog named Clifford. She lists all the reasons she likes Clifford and also the problems he causes. In the end she is happy with Clifford and decides he is the best for her.

The **Simple 6** ™ **FOCUS: Stick to the Topic: Pets**

PART II: **THE DRAWING**
          Draw Clifford.

Divide the paper into 4 boxes.
Start with a small hill in the upper right box.
In the lower left box, draw a big 2.
Add a backwards C to the 2 to make a paw.

Extend the C all the way to the left
Make a dot in the upper left box.
Use the dot for the tip of the tail.
Bring a curved tail down the left edge.
Slope down from the hill for his back.
Start the face with a capital U.
Add facial details.
Use 1s, backwards Cs, and commas for legs and paws.
Add ears and a collar.

PART III: THE ART PROJECT

Once your students learn to draw Clifford, the sky is the limit. Start with a simple drawing of Clifford and Emily Elizabeth. Talk to students about how a doghouse can be drawn in "the sky" and still end up being in the yard.

If you want to focus just on the head, draw Clifford's head, cut it out, and glue it behind a big, cutout doghouse that has a door that opens. Glue everything to a huge piece of paper. As part of the background, make a pile of bones for Clifford. Each one should have a new word on it from the story.

PART IV: THE WRITING CONNECTION

Games I Play with Clifford   Clifford Makes Mistakes   The Best Place to Hide
Clifford the Watchdog   The Best Pet in the World

also by Norman Bridwell . . .

PART 1   THE READ ALOUD: *Clifford's Manners* (1987)

Summary: Clifford has great manners. He says please, thank you, and excuse me. He follows the rules, he is a good sport, and he is also a helper. Everyone loves Clifford!

The Simple 6 ™ **FOCUS: Stick to the Topic: Good Manners**

PART II: ART PROJECT IDEA

Have each student draw Clifford on red construction paper. Outline the details with a black permanent marker. Give each student a large, white speech bubble to cut out. Write one of Clifford's rules for good manners in the bubble. Make each Clifford a part of a bulletin board about good manners.

PART III: THE WRITING CONNECTION

Clifford at the Movies   Clifford Cleans Up   Clifford Visits his Friends
Clifford Loses the Game   Clifford Teaches Good Manners to the Class

Other Clifford books . . .   *Clifford, the Small Red Puppy (1972, 1985)*
Clifford Visits the Hospital (2000)   *Clifford Takes a Trip (1995)*
Clifford's Tricks (1980)   *Clifford Keeps Cool (1999)*
Clifford and the Grouchy Neighbors (1980)   *Clifford's Class Trip (2003)*

Integrated Activities for Other Favorite Picture Books
THACHER HURD

PART 1: **THE READ ALOUD:** *Moo Cow Kaboom!* **by Thacher Hurd** (2003)

Summary: Farmer George's Moo Cow is cownapped by a Space Cowboy in the middle of the night. After being put in the Inter-Galactic Rodeo, Moo Cow's dancing skills get him back to Earth.

The Simple 6 ™ **FOCUS: Descriptive Sentences**

You won't find *went* or *said* in this book, even though it's for young readers and listeners. Look for all the precise verbs as you listen to or read this hilarious book!

PART II: **THE DRAWING**
Draw the cow.

This is a very simple drawing of a cow. Look for familiar shapes, numbers, and letters. Start with the head and go from there.

PART III: **ART PROJECT IDEA**
Of the books I have read, this is my number one choice for learning to draw a cow. Put this cow in the barnyard, on TV, at the zoo, or in space and you have the makings for another great story. Talk about the type of background you might need for each adventure. Take students through the background drawings step by step. Cows can be drawn in or drawn on other paper, cut out, and glued on.

PART IV: **THE WRITING CONNECTION**
Lost in Space
The Dancing Cow
Taken by Aliens
The Case of the Missing Cow

Integrated Activities for Other Favorite Picture Books
LEO LIONNI

PART 1:   THE READ ALOUD: *Frederick*, by Leo Lionni (1973)

Summary: While the little mice gather corn and nuts to prepare for winter, Frederick (the poet) gathers sunrays, colors, and words. His vivid descriptions of warmer seasons get the mice through the cold winter.

The Simple 6 ™   **FOCUS: Descriptive Sentences**

Frederick demonstrates the importance of observation, concentration, and remembering as he poetically describes his memories of the seasons.

PART II: THE DRAWING
Draw Frederick.

The paper collages in this book are aesthetically pleasing and wonderfully simple. Students need only torn and cut paper in two shades of gray to make Frederick. Texture is added with paint for background collage pieces. Wallpaper samples and plain construction paper could also be used.

PART III: ART PROJECT IDEA
Using the last page (full body) as an example, students should use paper, glue, and scissors to make Frederick. Point his right hand up instead of down. It can then "hold" your writing to share with the class.

PART IV: THE WRITING CONNECTION
Ode to Frederick
Winter, by Frederick and _____
Five Little Field Mice
Frederick the Poet
Limericks, by Frederick and _____
Sometimes I just Like to Sit and Think

Integrated Activities for Other Favorite Picture Books
ARNOLD LOBEL

Even though the Frog and Toad stories have been used as first grade readers rather than picture books, I include them here as another example of beloved characters in children's literature that have a powerful motivating factor for kids.

This example comes from **Frog and Toad Are Friends**.

PART 1   THE READ ALOUD: Frog and Toad are Friends: A Swim (1970)

Summary: Toad is embarrassed because he looks silly in his bathing suit. He dives into the river, but he won't come out because everyone will laugh. Just talking about it made all the animals curious, and of course, they laughed when he finally came out of the water. Toad went home in a huff.

The Simple 6™   FOCUS: Different Sentence Patterns

I like this book for different sentence patterns, because it exemplifies Lobel's unique, story-telling style. His text is entertaining, thoughtful, and always teaches some kind of lesson. While his sentences are short, he avoids the list-like, choppy quality with which students have a tendency to write.

PART II: THE DRAWING
         Draw Frog. Frog is tall and green.
         Draw Toad. Toad looks the same as Frog, but he is short and brown.

PART III: ART PROJECT IDEA
See the picture of Toad when he finally comes out of the water. He stands on a rock in his bathing suit. Draw Toad on the rock, but design your own bathing suit. Look at the picture of the turtle, lizards, snake, and field mouse on the next page. Put those laughing animals into the background of your picture.

PART IV: THE WRITING CONNECTION

The Day I Learned to Swim
Don't Look at Me
The Funniest Day of My Life
The Hilarious Swimsuit
Fun at the Creek
I Laughed So Hard that Day

Other Frog and Toad books . . .   *Frog and Toad Together (1971)*
Frog and Toad All Year (1976)
Days with Frog and Toad (1979)

Integrated Activities for Other Favorite Picture Books
ERIC CARLE

PART 1:   THE READ ALOUD: *The Very Hungry Caterpillar* (1981)

Summary: On Sunday a hungry caterpillar is born. As each day of the week goes by, he eats more and more. Finally, he builds a cocoon and emerges as a colorful butterfly!

The Simple 6 ™   **FOCUS: Logical Order**

The story is ordered by days of the week, but as each day passes, the caterpillar eats one more thing. Very short sentences with great transitions that explain the process of metamorphosis.

PART II: THE DRAWING
          Draw the caterpillar.

The caterpillar is a series of ovals. Have students practice drawing a series of identical ovals. Notice that the caterpillar's body is curved, not straight. How is the shape of the head different from the body segments? What details were added to make the caterpillar more interesting? Use crayons to draw the caterpillar.

PART III: ART PROJECT IDEA

Give each student a large sheet of construction paper on which to paint. Tape it to the desk or table so the corners don't curl up. Using tempra (green, yellow, blue) have them paint and texture their paper. The caterpillar on the cover has twenty body parts. While the paint is drying, ask young students to make a pattern for an oval out of tag board. (Paper should be about the size you would like the finished oval to be.) Show them how to trace ovals from their pattern onto the painted paper. Make sure they move from left to right, with ovals close to one another. Cut out the ovals. Keep one and share the rest with their classmates. They will do the same. The teacher can paint several pieces of construction paper with red. Give each student a rectangle the approximate size of the head. They can draw or trace before they cut it out, and add the details with their scraps.

PART IV: THE WRITING CONNECTION

How I Became a Butterfly

What I'd Do with Only 7 Days

The Day I Became a Butterfly

I Ate the Whole Thing!

I am Beautiful!

My Favorite Food

My Journey Through Life

Other Eric Carle books . . .   *Do You Want to Be My Friend? (1988)*

                                                   Papa, Please Get the Moon for Me (1991)

                                                   The Mixed-up Chameleon (1993)

                                                   The Grouchy Ladybug (1996)

PICTURE BOOKS WITH EASY-TO-DRAW CHARACTERS

PART 1:   THE READ ALOUD:

Summary:

The Simple 6 ™   FOCUS:

PART II: THE DRAWING

PART III: ART PROJECT IDEA

PART IV: THE WRITING CONNECTION

Other books by this author:

Chapter 3 Assessment for Beginning Artists and Authors

Assessment Across the District

Assessment in the Classroom

Defining Expectations for Beginning Writers in Your School

Tracking Progress in K-2

Scoring Kindergarten Writing/Drawing Samples
KDG: Baseline Expectations
Prompt: Me/Anchor Papers
Expectations Throughout the Year
Prompt: My Home 1st Semester Anchor Papers
                      2nd Semester Anchor Papers

Scoring Student Writing/Drawing Samples in Grade 1
GR 1: Baseline Expectations
Prompt: My Family/Anchor Papers
Expectations Throughout the Year
Prompt: My Fun Day 1st Semester Anchor Papers
                       2nd Semester Anchor Papers

GR 2: Baseline Expectations
Prompt: Being a Good Friend/Anchor Papers
Moving into Formal Assessment During the Second Semester

The Simple 6™ Poster

Chapter 3   Assessment for Beginning Artists and Authors

All writing and drawing is not assessed or brought to publication. However, there are times when assessment is necessary – or reporting student progress on a report card as well as for school improvement documentation.

Assessment Across the District

Formal writing assessment is something that many teachers dread. To make it a more positive experience, teachers need training, practice sessions, and time to collaborate with their peers. If formal quarterly writing assessments are being implemented district wide, it's a good idea to start with one prompt at each grade level that will be used by all schools. The prompt format and testing scenario should match your state's requirements. Once the initial prompt and procedure have had a trial run, it's easier to see things that may need to be adjusted.

Teachers appreciate being reminded at the beginning of the assessment month, so they can allow time for the task as they design lesson plans. Have students do the writing two to three weeks prior to the end so teachers can use the scores as part of their quarterly classroom assessment as well. Allow a one-week window for giving the prompt, and allow another week window for scoring the prompt. All papers should be scored with a mini rubric, and all scores should be transferred to a Class Analysis Sheet and turned in by the Friday of the scoring week.

The school administrator or writing chair should then compile data. Analysis of all school data should be shared with staff members by the following Friday. This reporting of data falls into the same category as homework. If you don't have time to grade it and promptly return it, don't assign it. By the same token, if teachers are being asked to assign and grade within a specific time frame, they should be entitled to data analysis in a timely fashion as well. It's takes less than five minutes at a staff meeting to update everyone regarding progress on building goals. Do it.

In large districts, this information should then be transferred from building administrator to central office. All schools are then charted and compared. A brief analysis should be included, as well as plans for intervention.

Time Table:

Week 1:

Students write from the same prompt at each grade level.

Week 2:

Teachers score the writing samples and complete the Class Analysis Chart. A copy of the chart is due in the school office by Friday.

Week 3:

Administrators compile and analyze the data, reporting to teachers by Friday. A copy of the data analysis is due in central office by Friday.

Week 4:

Central office administrator compiles data from each school. Analysis (and plans for intervention) are returned to each school by Friday.

Assessment in the Classroom

Assessment for instructional purposes hopefully occurs more often than local assessment for a school improvement plan. Schedule it, and stick to it. At Grade 2, I recommend formal assessment four times each (nine-week) grading period. At Grade 1, two formal assessments might be given each quarter. For Kindergarten students, one formal assessment each quarter is probably sufficient. Assign a writing topic or prompt idea that closely resembles your state format. Remember to relate writing topics to what you are studying.

The K-2 Assessment Dilemma

While standards dictate instructional focus, standardized assessment guides grade level expectations. Because statewide testing typically starts in Grade 3 or Grade 4 there isn't a standardized format for measuring levels of achievement at the early grades. The amount of progress made each quarter and the change in expectation throughout the school year complicates matters further.

Because children come to school with such varied experiences, it is very difficult to set generic standards for every teacher in grades K-2. Instead, guiding teachers through the process of setting their own quarterly goals and expectations is much more beneficial. These expectations are then used as guidelines for scoring.

Comparing Data for Grades K-2

Another realization with young students is that because the bar is raised so often and so much from beginning to end, it's impossible to measure growth by comparing numbers only. For example, in the upper grades you might have a student who starts the year with a Score 2 on a writing sample. Throughout the year, you may be able to bring this student to the Score 4 range. Growth is obvious because the rubric expectations do not change throughout the year. At the K-2 level, however, the expectation changes every quarter. Therefore, a student who starts with a Score 2 and ends with a Score 4 has obviously made progress. What has to be considered, though, is the student who starts at a Score 4 and ends at a Score 4. That student has made progress also, in keeping up with the pace throughout the year and maintaining a "passing" level.

Defining Expectations

The chart on the following page can serve as a guide while working with colleagues to articulate expectations for K-2 growth. Teachers at each grade level should discuss realistic expectations for the type of students in the school district. After each grade level has made tentative decisions, come together to see if the goals are well articulated – does the goal at the end of Kindergarten match or slightly overlap the expectation for baseline Grade 1?

Defining Expectations for
Beginning Writers in Your School

GRADE 2

Final	W: 8-sentence story Topic/Order/Words Patterns/Details/Audience
3rd Q: March	Simple 6™ Implementation
2nd Q: December	Final Simple 6™ Writing/Drawing Assessment W: 8-sentence story Topic/Order/Patterns/Details-Feelings P: Topic/Details or Background
Baseline	W: 5-sentence story Topic/Order/Patterns/Details-Feelings P: Topic/Details or Background

GRADE 1
Simple 6™: Writing/Drawing

Final	W: 5-8 sentence story Topic/Order/Patterns/Details-Feelings P: Topic/Details or Background
2nd Q: December	W: 3 complete sentences Topic/Order/Details-Feelings P: Topic/Details or Background
Baseline	W: 1 complete sentence Topic/Order/Details-Feelings P: Topic/Details or Background

KINDERGARTEN
Simple 6™: Writing/Drawing

Final	W: 2-3 complete sentences Topic/Order/Details-Feelings P: Topic/Recog./Details-Feelings
2nd Q: December	W: 1 complete sentence Topic/Order P: Topic/Recog./Details or Background
Baseline	W: first name P: Topic/Recog./Details or Background

Defining Expectations for
Beginning Writers in Your School

GRADE 2

Final	Simple 6™: Formal Assessment
3rd Q: March	Simple 6™: Implementation
2nd Q: December	Final Simple 6™ W/D Assessment
1st Q: October	
Baseline	

GRADE 1

Simple 6™: Writing/Drawing

Final	
3rd Q: March	
2nd Q: December	
1st Q: October	
Baseline	

KINDERGARTEN

Simple 6™: Writing/Drawing

Final	
3rd Q: March	
2nd Q: December	
1st Q: October	
Baseline	

For Consideration . . .

Simplified Writing Expectations 2-K
(work back from Grade 3 expectations)

Grade 2

End	8+ Sentence Story	Topic/BME/Patterns Details/Interesting Words/Audience
Middle	Simple 6™ Implementation	
Baseline	5+ Sentence Story	Topic/BME/Details or Feelings

Grade 1

End	7-8 Sentence Story	Topic/BME/Patterns Details or Feelings
Middle	5 Sentence Story	Topic/BME/Details
Baseline	2-3 Sentence Story	Topic/BME

Kindergarten

End	2-3 Sentence Story	Topic/ Patterns Details or Feelings
Middle	1 Complete sentence	Topic
Baseline	First Name	

Tracking Progress in K-2

On the following pages are the tools you will need for scoring and data collection.

The Mini Rubric

Use the mini rubric to score papers. There is a Kindergarten rubric as well as a Grade 1/ Beginning Grade 2 rubric.

The Simple 6 ™

0 / 1

____ DRAWING: Stick to the Topic
____ DRAWING: Recognizable
____ DRAWING: Details or Background
____ WRITING: Stick to the Topic
____ WRITING: Logical Order
____ WRITING: Details or Feelings

____ TOTAL   KINDERGARTEN

©Kay Davidson, 2006

Class Analysis Chart

Complete a Class Analysis Chart to see what skills need to be revisited. Keep these in a folder to help guide classroom instruction.

	Drawing			Writing			
NAMES	Topic	Recognizable	Details	Topic	Order	Details or Feelings	TOTAL

Yearly Class Record

Transfer data to the K-2 Yearly Class Record for writing/drawing progress. This, along with your completed Expectations Chart will become the documentation for your school improvement plan. Copies should also be forwarded to the next year's teachers. See p. 157.

WRITING PROMPTS CLASS RECORD

YEAR _____ TEACHER _____

STUDENT NAME	BASELINE: AUG CONT (6)/CONV (4)	PROMPT 1: OCT. CONT (6)/CONV (4)	PROMPT 2: JAN CONT (6)/CONV (4)	PROMPT 3: MAR. CONT (6)/CONV (4)	FINAL: MAY CONT (6)/CONV (4)

The Simple6™

0 / 1

_____ DRAWING: Stick to the Topic
_____ DRAWING: Recognizable
_____ DRAWING: Details or Background
_____ WRITING: Stick to the Topic
_____ WRITING: Logical Order
_____ WRITING: Details or Feelings

_____ TOTAL KINDERGARTEN

©Kay Davidson, 2006

The Simple6™

0 / 1

_____ DRAWING: Stick to the Topic
_____ DRAWING: Recognizable
_____ DRAWING: Details or Background
_____ WRITING: Stick to the Topic
_____ WRITING: Logical Order
_____ WRITING: Details or Feelings

_____ TOTAL KINDERGARTEN

©Kay Davidson, 2006

The Simple6™

0 / 1

_____ DRAWING: Stick to the Topic
_____ DRAWING: Recognizable
_____ DRAWING: Details or Background
_____ WRITING: Stick to the Topic
_____ WRITING: Logical Order
_____ WRITING: Details or Feelings

_____ TOTAL KINDERGARTEN

©Kay Davidson, 2006

The Simple6™

0 / 1

_____ DRAWING: Stick to the Topic
_____ DRAWING: Recognizable
_____ DRAWING: Details or Background
_____ WRITING: Stick to the Topic
_____ WRITING: Logical Order
_____ WRITING: Details or Feelings

_____ TOTAL KINDERGARTEN

©Kay Davidson, 2006

Class Analysis Chart
for Kindergarten

Prompt _____ Date _____

NAMES	Drawing			Writing			
	Topic	Recog-nizable	Details or Background	Topic	Order	Details or Feelings	TOTAL

Comments

The Simple 6 ™

Grades 1 and 2

0 / 1
___ DRAWING: Stick to the Topic
___ DRAWING: Details or Background
___ WRITING: Stick to the Topic
___ WRITING: Logical Order
___ WRITING: Sentence Patterns
___ WRITING: Details or Feelings

___ TOTAL

©Kay Davidson, 2006

The Simple 6 ™

Grades 1 and 2

0 / 1
___ DRAWING: Stick to the Topic
___ DRAWING: Details or Background
___ WRITING: Stick to the Topic
___ WRITING: Logical Order
___ WRITING: Sentence Patterns
___ WRITING: Details or Feelings

___ TOTAL

©Kay Davidson, 2006

The Simple 6 ™

Grades 1 and 2

0 / 1
___ DRAWING: Stick to the Topic
___ DRAWING: Details or Background
___ WRITING: Stick to the Topic
___ WRITING: Logical Order
___ WRITING: Sentence Patterns
___ WRITING: Details or Feelings

___ TOTAL

©Kay Davidson, 2006

The Simple 6 ™

Grades 1 and 2

0 / 1
___ DRAWING: Stick to the Topic
___ DRAWING: Details or Background
___ WRITING: Stick to the Topic
___ WRITING: Logical Order
___ WRITING: Sentence Patterns
___ WRITING: Details or Feelings

___ TOTAL

©Kay Davidson, 2006

Class Analysis Chart
for Grade 1 and Beginning Grade 2

Prompt _____ Date _____

| | Drawing | | Writing | | | | |
NAMES	Topic	Recog-nizable	Topic	Order	Patterns	Details or Feelings	TOTAL

Comments

Scoring Kindergarten Writing/Drawing Samples

Begin at the Beginning

Collect a baseline sample. What do your new students know about writing and drawing before they know you? Students with high-ability levels, early childhood nurturing, and a variety of life experiences may come to you with reading, drawing, and writing skills. You may also have students who don't speak in complete sentences and who don't know which way the pages in a book should be turned.

A baseline writing/drawing sample not only gives you diagnostic information about cognitive skills, but it will immediately give you a vast amount of information about your students' social skills, listening ability, and independent work habits. Take notes on a clipboard as students engage in this first activity. The following chart offers *suggestions* for baseline Kindergarten:

	Suggested Expectations for Kindergarten Baseline Writing/Drawing Samples	
	Drawing	Writing
Score 6	picture has details	Sticks to the topic, has logical order, and includes details / feelings
Score 5	picture has details	Sticks to the topic and has order or details
Score 4	picture may have details	Sticks to the topic and may have order, details, or feelings
Score 3	recognizable picture	attempts to Stick to the Topic
Score 2	recognizable picture	scribble writing
Score 1	low-level attempt	no attempt/scribble writing

Following is an example of a prompt you might use as a baseline. Attach a Kindergarten mini rubric for scoring purposes.

> Kindergarten Baseline Writing/Drawing: ME

Me

I am happy that you are in my class. I am making a book with everyone's picture in it! What is your name? What do you look like? What makes you look special and different from everyone else?

Draw a picture of yourself in the box below. Be sure to put in as many details as you can.

On the next page, write a story about yourself. Describe what you look like. Tell me your name.

TOPIC: Me

Writing Sample
(nonsense letters included in drawing)

The **Simple 6** ™ **Mini Rubric**

0 / 1

_1_ DRAWING: Stick to the Topic
___ DRAWING: Recognizable
___ DRAWING: Details
___ WRITING: Stick to the Topic
___ WRITING: Logical Order
___ WRITING: Details or Feelings

_1_ TOTAL   KINDERGARTEN

Explanation:
    If I didn't know the topic, would I describe this picture as a drawing of a Kindergarten child? Because my answer is "no," I give one point for attempting to stick to the topic in the drawing. No points are given for attempting to write letters or "scribble writing."

TOPIC: Me

Score 2

Writing Sample
(writing included in drawing)

The Simple 6 ™ Mini Rubric

0 / 1
_1_   DRAWING: Stick to the Topic
_1_   DRAWING: Recognizable
___   DRAWING: Details
___   WRITING: Stick to the Topic
___   WRITING: Logical Order
___   WRITING: Details or Feelings

_2_   TOTAL   KINDERGARTEN

Explanation:
    The student sticks to the topic by drawing a picture of himself. It is recognizable as a person. He attempts to write his name, but no point is given for writing because it is part of the picture, is not on the story paper, and is intended for ownership purposes.

TOPIC: Me

Writing Sample

Casandra
yellow
I c yellow dr

 **Simple6** ™ **Mini Rubric**

0 / 1
_1_   DRAWING: Stick to the Topic
_1_   DRAWING: Recognizable
___   DRAWING: Details
_1_   WRITING: Stick to the Topic
___   WRITING: Logical Order
___   WRITING: Details or Feelings

_3_   TOTAL   KINDERGARTEN

Explanation:
    Casandra's picture of herself is recognizable, even though we can't tell if it is a boy or girl. She has attempted to stick to the topic by writing her name and telling us that something about her is yellow.

TOPIC: Me

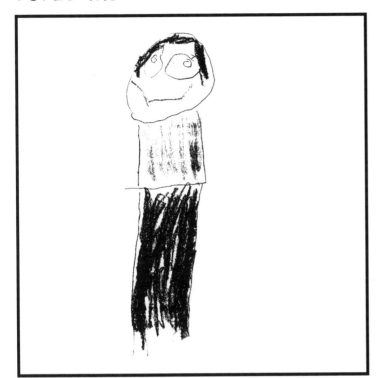

Writing Sample

Kasey	I hav a Bn Rm	I am a cwboy	I hav Bon hor
I like GhlE	I am 6 my Brday NovBr fiftt		I like black

The Simple 6 ™ Mini Rubric

0 / 1

_1_ DRAWING: Stick to the Topic
_1_ DRAWING: Recognizable
___ DRAWING: Details
_1_ WRITING: Stick to the Topic
___ WRITING: Logical Order
_1_ WRITING: Details or Feelings

_4_ TOTAL   KINDERGARTEN

Explanation:

We can easily see Kasey in the picture, although there are few details. From the writing, we know he is 6, is a cowboy, has brown hair, has a birthday on November 5, and likes black. He has stuck to the topic in his writing and has given many details. Inventive spelling is close enough for us to figure out what he is trying to say. In a Score 4 paper (passing) no points are given for attempts.

TOPIC: Me

Writing Sample

Kendra I a msix. I like redandblue.
I like my cat

The Simple 6™ Mini Rubric

0 / 1
_1_   DRAWING: Stick to the Topic
_1_   DRAWING: Recognizable
_1_   DRAWING: Details
_____   WRITING: Stick to the Topic
_1_   WRITING: Logical Order
_1_   WRITING: Details or Feelings

_5_   TOTAL   KINDERGARTEN

Explanation:
   It is easy to see that this is a girl because of her skirt, her pigtails, and the heart on her shirt. Note the inclusion of feet and hands, even though there are more than five fingers. Writing is well done, but it does not describe what she looks like, which was the topic. As the score gets closer to a 6, prompt instructions must be followed exactly.

TOPIC: Me

Writing Sample

Riley
my haR is BROWN
my IAZ R gREEN

The Simple 6 ™ Mini Rubric

0 / 1
_1_ DRAWING: Stick to the Topic
_1_ DRAWING: Recognizable
_1_ DRAWING: Details
_1_ WRITING: Stick to the Topic
_1_ WRITING: Logical Order
_1_ WRITING: Details or Feelings

_6_ TOTAL   KINDERGARTEN

Explanation:
    Riley draws a picture of herself that is easily recognizable. It includes details such as irises in the eyes, eyebrows and lashes, lips, fingers, shoes, and puffy sleeves on the dress. The writing describes her, the words are in order to make complete sentences, and she has included details, making this a low score 6 — only because of length and lack of additional detail in the writing.

TOPIC: Me

Writing Sample

My name is Hanna. I have brown
hair and blue iis. I like to go to the
mooll. I have 3 dog and I have a cat
and I have 6 kitins. My Brtday is Oc-
tober the 28.

The Simple 6 ™ Mini Rubric

0 / 1

_1_ DRAWING: Stick to the Topic
_1_ DRAWING: Recognizable
_1_ DRAWING: Details
_1_ WRITING: Stick to the Topic
_1_ WRITING: Logical Order
_1_ WRITING: Details or Feelings

_6_ TOTAL   KINDERGARTEN

Explanation:
    Hanna has a very sophisticated picture
for kindergarten. Note the sleeves and
the detail on the clothing. Her writing includes details about what she looks like as
well as other bits of information you might
want to know about her. Sentence structure and actual development of a paragraph are outstanding, especially for the
beginning of the year.

Suggestions for Defining Average
Expectations throughout the Kindergarten Year
(What would you like students to be able to do?)

Baseline: Stick to the topic. Follow directions.
Draw a picture, holding the crayon or pencil correctly.
Write your first name.
Write as much as possible about the topic.

Midyear: Stick to the topic. Follow directions.
Draw a recognizable picture.
Include some details or background.
Attempt to write at least one sentence with invented or real spelling.

Final: Stick to the topic. Follow directions.
Draw a detailed picture.
Write one to two sentences about the topic.

```
The
  Simple6  ™  Mini Rubric

0 / 1
____     DRAWING:  Stick to the Topic
____     DRAWING:  Recognizable
____     DRAWING:  Details
____     WRITING:  Stick to the Topic
____     WRITING:  Logical Order
____     WRITING:  Details or Feelings

____     TOTAL         KINDERGARTEN
```

The following writing/drawing prompt, My Home, is followed by two sets of student anchor papers. The first set was scored with first semester expectations. The second set was scored with second semester expectations. Again, these are just suggestions. Your school or district should determine the actual anchor papers. The type of students you have in your school or district will determine the Kindergarten expectations.

My Home

Homes come in many different shapes, colors, and sizes. What does your home look like? What color is it? What is near your home?

Draw a picture of your home in the box below. Be sure to put in as many details as you can.

On the next page, write a story about your home.

TOPIC: My Home

Writing Sample

(misc. letters)

The Simple 6 ™ Mini Rubric

0 / 1
_1_ DRAWING: Stick to the Topic
___ DRAWING: Recognizable
___ DRAWING: Details
___ WRITING: Stick to the Topic
___ WRITING: Logical Order
___ WRITING: Details or Feelings

_1_ TOTAL   KINDERGARTEN

Explanation:
   Jimmy attempts the drawing, but it is not recognizable as his home. He is able to write his name, but the rest of the story is a series of nonsense letters.

TOPIC: My Home

Writing Sample

I F V EUASF.
I KAMB V.
In n mem.

The Simple 6 ™ Mini Rubric

0 / 1
_1__ DRAWING: Stick to the Topic
_1__ DRAWING: Recognizable
____ DRAWING: Details
____ WRITING: Stick to the Topic
____ WRITING: Logical Order
____ WRITING: Details or Feelings

_2_ TOTAL   KINDERGARTEN

Explanation:
This Score 2 sample gets a point for sticking to the topic in the drawing and making the house recognizable. Without a roof or background, it does not get a third point for details. The door and windows are what makes it recognizable as a house and not a box. No point is given for nonsense writing.

TOPIC: My Home

Writing Sample

zs is me
2540518

The Simple 6 ™ Mini Rubric

```
0 / 1
_1_    DRAWING:  Stick to the Topic
_1_    DRAWING:  Recognizable
_1__   DRAWING:  Details
___    WRITING:  Stick to the Topic
___    WRITING:  Logical Order
___    WRITING:  Details or Feelings

_3__   TOTAL        KINDERGARTEN
```

Explanation:
    This Score 3 gets points on the drawing for sticking to the topic, having a home that is recognizable, and details such as window panes, a door, a pointed roof, and what appear to be trees or bushes. The numbers seem to represent her address but may be her phone number.

TOPIC: My Home

Writing Sample

ZAC
mi home

The Simple 6 ™ **Mini Rubric**

0 / 1

_1_	DRAWING:	Stick to the Topic
_1_	DRAWING:	Recognizable
_1_	DRAWING:	Details
_1_	WRITING:	Stick to the Topic
___	WRITING:	Logical Order
___	WRITING:	Details or Feelings
_4_	TOTAL	KINDERGARTEN

Explanation:
   For such seemingly low developmental skills, this picture is loaded with details! People in the window, the fence, the flower, the swingset, the grill, and the mailbox on the street tell me that Zac looks at the world critically and has a great recollection of details. One point is given for sticking to the topic in his writing.

TOPIC: My Home

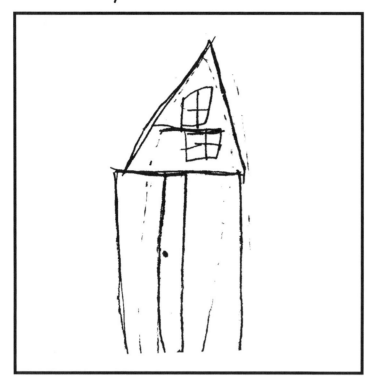

Writing Sample

My Home is BiG.

The Simple 6 ™ Mini Rubric

0 / 1

_1_ DRAWING: Stick to the Topic
_1_ DRAWING: Recognizable
___ DRAWING: Details
_1_ WRITING: Stick to the Topic
_1_ WRITING: Logical Order
_1_ WRITING: Details or Feelings

_5_ TOTAL   KINDERGARTEN

Explanation:
   The house is recognizable, but not enough details and/or background are given for the third drawing point. Writing sticks to the topic, words are in order, and the sentence is descriptive.

TOPIC: My Home

Writing Sample

Spencer
My Home is a rokeT. it HaS a GarGe.

The **Simple6** ™ **Mini Rubric**

0 / 1
_1__ DRAWING: Stick to the Topic
_1__ DRAWING: Recognizable
_1__ DRAWING: Details
_1__ WRITING: Stick to the Topic
_1__ WRITING: Logical Order
_1__ WRITING: Details or Feelings

_6__ TOTAL   KINDERGARTEN

Explanation:
    Complete with a planet in the upper corner and lots of stars, this is an outstanding piece for a beginning Kindergarten student.

Increasing Expectations for Second Semester

The following student samples suggest expectations for scoring as the year progresses. Again, it is important to determine your own expectations as you articulate writing goals for K-2 with your colleagues.

TOPIC: My Home

SECOND SEMESTER
Kindergarten
Student Sample
Liz

Score 1

Writing Sample

LIZ MOMA
L   laE / IZB / l   l

The Simple 6™ Mini Rubric

0 / 1

_1_	DRAWING:	Stick to the Topic
___	DRAWING:	Recognizable
___	DRAWING:	Details
___	WRITING:	Stick to the Topic
___	WRITING:	Logical Order
___	WRITING:	Details or Feelings
_1_	TOTAL	KINDERGARTEN

Explanation:
   Liz attempts to stick to the topic by drawing a rectangle that we assume is her home.

TOPIC: My Home

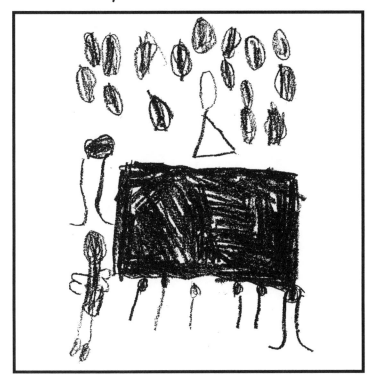

Writing Sample

Joe

The Simple 6 ™ Mini Rubric

0 / 1

_1_	DRAWING:	Stick to the Topic
___	DRAWING:	Recognizable
_1_	DRAWING:	Details
___	WRITING:	Stick to the Topic
___	WRITING:	Logical Order
___	WRITING:	Details or Feelings
_2_	TOTAL	KINDERGARTEN

Explanation:
 Two points for this drawing because while he attempts to stick to the topic and includes details such as clouds, trees, and people, we don't really recognize the black rectangle as a house. The writing consisted of his name only.

TOPIC: My Home

Writing Sample

I Home
White

The Simple 6 ™ Mini Rubric

0 / 1
_1_   DRAWING: Stick to the Topic
_1_   DRAWING: Recognizable
_1_   DRAWING: Details
___   WRITING: Stick to the Topic
___   WRITING: Logical Order
___   WRITING: Details or Feelings

_3_   TOTAL   KINDERGARTEN

Explanation:
    Points are given for sticking to the topic in the drawing, being recognizable as a home, and having details such as a tree, clouds, sky, a door, curtains in the windows, shingles on the roof, and a swingset. Writing was attempted, but no points are given for year end.

TOPIC: My Home

Writing Sample

my Home H o m esi Crwn.

The **Simple6** ™ **Mini Rubric**

0 / 1

_1_	DRAWING:	Stick to the Topic
_1_	DRAWING:	Recognizable
_1_	DRAWING:	Details
_1_	WRITING:	Stick to the Topic
___	WRITING:	Logical Order
___	WRITING:	Details or Feelings

_4_   TOTAL   KINDERGARTEN

Explanation:

Jolene's home is recognizable and has details such as a roof, windows, a door, flowers, and sky. We assume Jolene is in the yard. One point is given for sticking to the topic in the writing, even though we aren't sure what is being said about her home.

TOPIC: My Home

Writing Sample

My home is big. It haves 24 windos in it. I love my home.
it's the best it haves lots of rooms in it. The toy room is best
becus it haves ol of the toy in the toy room. My bed is
veary cufy.

The Simple 6 ™ Mini Rubric

0 / 1

_1__ DRAWING: Stick to the Topic
_1__ DRAWING: Recognizable
___ DRAWING: Details
_1__ WRITING: Stick to the Topic
_1__ WRITING: Logical Order
_1__ WRITING: Details or Feelings

_5_ TOTAL   KINDERGARTEN

Explanation:
   With a few more details in
the picture, this would have been
a Score 6 paper for a Kindergarten student.

TOPIC: My Home

Writing Sample

I live in a house. My house is in Kewnna. My house is big and gray. It has a atick and a basemit. It has a chimney. It has a door and a roof. My favort room in my house is my bedroom. four people live in my house.

The Simple 6 ™ Mini Rubric

0 / 1

_1__	DRAWING: Stick to the Topic
_1__	DRAWING: Recognizable
_1__	DRAWING: Details
_1__	WRITING: Stick to the Topic
_1__	WRITING: Logical Order
_1__	WRITING: Details or Feelings

_6__   TOTAL   KINDERGARTEN

Explanation:
   The girl in the picture has no hands. Other than that, this end-of-year sample is outstanding!

Scoring Student Writing/Drawing Samples in Grade 1

Begin at the Beginning. . .again!

Students come to 1st grade with various experiences and backgrounds. They may have attended full day Kindergarten, ½ day Kindergarten, day care, preschool, home school, or home care. It's important to determine students' levels as early as possible.

Collect a baseline sample. What do your new students know about writing and drawing before they know you? Are they looking at you as you give instructions? How do they hold the pencil or crayon? Do they begin drawing as soon as they know what to do? Do they stay on task? Do they use upper and lower case letters in their writing? Do they depend on others for ideas?

A baseline writing/drawing sample not only gives you diagnostic information about cognitive skills, but it will immediately give you a vast amount of information about your students' social habits, listening skills, and attention span.

Suggested Expectations for Grade 1 Baseline Writing/Drawing Samples		
Score 6	picture has many details	Sticks to the topic, has logical order, details/feelings, and has different sentence patterns.
Score 5	picture has details	Sticks to the topic, has logical order, details/feelings
Score 4	picture may have details	Sticks to the topic, may have logical order, and probably includes details/feelings
Score 3	picture may have details	Sticks to the topic, has logical order, OR details/feelings
Score 2	recognizable picture	Sticks to the topic
Score 1	attempts picture	OR attempts to stick to the topic

On the next page is an example of a prompt you might use as a baseline. It uses the Grade 1 mini rubric on page 71. When completed, it should be attached to the student sample.

Grade 1 Baseline Writing/Drawing: My Family

My Family

Our family is very important to us. How many people are in your family? Who are they? What do they look like?

Draw a picture and write a sentence or story about your family. Be sure to show what each person looks like.

On the next page, write a story about your family.

Topic: My Family

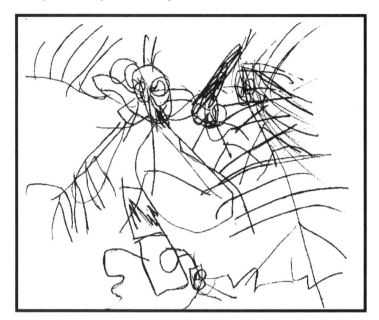

Writing Sample

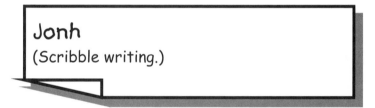

Jonh
(Scribble writing.)

The Simple 6 ™ **Mini Rubric**

0 / 1
_1_   DRAWING: Stick to the Topic
___   DRAWING: Details
___   WRITING: Stick to the Topic
___   WRITING: Logical Order
___   WRITING: Sentence Patterns
___   WRITING: Details or Feelings

_1_   TOTAL   Grade 1

Explanation:
   We give the student the benefit of the doubt, assuming he is attempting to draw a picture of his family. The question I always ask is, "If I didn't know the topic, would I recognize what this is?" I would have to say no for Grade 1. No points are given for writing, which was scribbled and undecipherable.

Writing Sample

Payton
My family I hav 4 Darnell I family member

The Simple 6 ™ Mini Rubric

0 / 1
_1_ DRAWING: Stick to the Topic
___ DRAWING: Details
_1_ WRITING: Stick to the Topic
___ WRITING: Logical Order
___ WRITING: Sentence Patterns
___ WRITING: Details or Feelings

_2_ TOTAL Grade 1

Explanation:
We assume that the four stick figures are family members. There are not enough details to tell one from the next. In the writing, we see the word family so he gets the point for attempting to stick to the topic. No other points are given.

Writing Sample

Kita
I am kapem wof mi fle bekus it is fum to do

The Simple 6 ™ Mini Rubric

0 / 1
_1_ DRAWING: Stick to the Topic
_1_ DRAWING: Details
___ WRITING: Stick to the Topic
___ WRITING: Logical Order
___ WRITING: Sentence Patterns
_1_ WRITING: Details or Feelings

_3_ TOTAL   Grade 1

Explanation:
    We assume that there are five people in Kita's family. Since we know they are camping, we see a tent, a blanket, and their car. However, the focus was on what the family looked like, and they all look alike.

Topic: My Family

Writing Sample

Michael
My family is nice. There are five people in my family.
When we are together we play outside.

The Simple 6™ Mini Rubric

0 / 1
_1_   DRAWING: Stick to the Topic
_1_   DRAWING: Details
___   WRITING: Stick to the Topic
_1_   WRITING: Logical Order
___   WRITING: Sentence Patterns
_1_   WRITING: Details or Feelings

_4_   TOTAL   Grade 1

Explanation:
   Both points were given for drawing, although improvement would be expected on the people throughout the year. He gets writing points for logical order, because the words are in order to make sentences. He also gets the point for details. However, his story does not answer the questions in the prompt. No point is given for sticking to the topic.
   (This paper passes, so there are now stricter parameters.)

Topic: My Family

Writing Sample

Lexi
My family is special. There are four people in my family. Mom
Dad Kylah and me. I feel great about my family a lot.

The Simple 6™ Mini Rubric

0 / 1
_1_ DRAWING: Stick to the Topic
_1_ DRAWING: Details
_1_ WRITING: Stick to the Topic
_1_ WRITING: Logical Order
___ WRITING: Sentence Patterns
_1_ WRITING: Details or Feelings

_5_ TOTAL Grade 1

Explanation:
   Great family portrait with more sophistication in the drawing. Work on ears, shoelaces, and buttons or designs on T-shirts. Writing points are given for topic, order, and descriptions. For revision, have her focus on what the people look like.

Topic: My Family

Writing Sample

Lauren
My family is gerate!! Did you know that I have 5 peopl in my family? My Mom Dad and my sister and my baby brother. Wen we are together we look like a fantastik family. I Love my wunderful family!

The Simple 6™ Mini Rubric

0 / 1
_1_ DRAWING: Stick to the Topic
_1_ DRAWING: Details
_1_ WRITING: Stick to the Topic
_1_ WRITING: Logical Order
_1_ WRITING: Sentence Patterns
_1_ WRITING: Details or Feelings

_6_ TOTAL   Grade 1

Explanation:
   This is an outstanding paper for a Grade 1 baseline. The drawing not only has detailed people, but they are in a room with furniture. She has a beginning, details in the middle, and an end to her story. She includes three sentence patterns (as well as some interesting words!)

Assessment in Grade 1

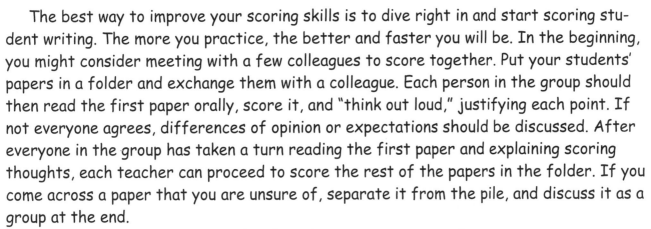

The best way to improve your scoring skills is to dive right in and start scoring student writing. The more you practice, the better and faster you will be. In the beginning, you might consider meeting with a few colleagues to score together. Put your students' papers in a folder and exchange them with a colleague. Each person in the group should then read the first paper orally, score it, and "think out loud," justifying each point. If not everyone agrees, differences of opinion or expectations should be discussed. After everyone in the group has taken a turn reading the first paper and explaining scoring thoughts, each teacher can proceed to score the rest of the papers in the folder. If you come across a paper that you are unsure of, separate it from the pile, and discuss it as a group at the end.

In situations where all grade-level students are writing to the same prompt, you may want to develop a set of anchor papers that will be used as guides in future years. Measuring growth throughout the year is important. Here are some guidelines for increasing the level of expectation throughout the Grade 1 year.

**Suggestions for Defining Average Expectations
Throughout the Grade 1 Year
(What would you like students to be able to do?)**

Baseline: Stick to the topic. Follow directions.
Draw a detailed picture, holding the pencil correctly.
Write your full name correctly.
Write at least one complete sentence about the topic that contains details or feelings.

Midyear: Stick to the topic. Follow directions.
Draw a detailed picture.
Write at least three to five sentences that stick to the topic, have a beginning / middle / end, and include details and/or feelings.

Final: Stick to the topic. Follow directions.
Draw a detailed picture.
Write at least five to eight sentences that stick to the topic, have a beginning / middle / end, and include details and/or feelings. Include statements, questions, and/or exclamations.

The following Baseline/Final anchor papers from the prompt, My Fun Day, compare the difference in scoring expectations between samples done during the first semester and samples done in the second semester. The same students did not do the comparison samples.

My Fun Day

Think of a fun day you had in the past few weeks. What did you do on that day? Who was with you? Did you do something special, or did you just have an ordinary fun day?

Draw a picture and write a story about your fun day. Be sure to show and tell about what you did.

On the next page, write a story about your fun day.

Topic: My Fun Day

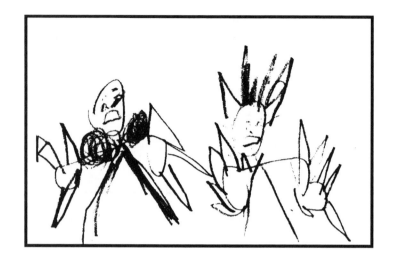

Writing Sample

No writing was attempted.

The Simple 6™ Mini Rubric

0 / 1

_1_	DRAWING:	Stick to the Topic
___	DRAWING:	Details
___	WRITING:	Stick to the Topic
___	WRITING:	Logical Order
___	WRITING:	Sentence Patterns
___	WRITING:	Details or Feelings
_1_	TOTAL	GRADE 1

Explanation:
   We assume that the two stick figures are having fun. There are not enough details to give us an idea of what they are doing. No writing was attempted.

Topic: My Fun Day

Writing Sample

Jeffrey
My fun they yus the prk I WNT dowon slid

The Simple6 ™ Mini Rubric

0 / 1		
att 1	DRAWING:	Stick to the Topic
___	DRAWING:	Details
att 1	WRITING:	Stick to the Topic
___	WRITING:	Logical Order
___	WRITING:	Sentence Patterns
___	WRITING:	Details or Feelings
_2_	TOTAL	GRADE 1

Explanation:
   We assume that the stick figures are Jeffrey and his dad. This is a very low-level drawing for Grade 1, but he has attempted the task. He also gets one point for attempting the writing task. We see the words fun and park, and we understand that he is going down the slide.

Topic: My Fun Day

Writing Sample

Brittney
I had a fun day before. I jrived griampalls chratr.

The Simple 6 ™ Mini Rubric

0 / 1
_1_ DRAWING: Stick to the Topic
_1_ DRAWING: Details
_1_ WRITING: Stick to the Topic
____ WRITING: Logical Order
____ WRITING: Sentence Patterns
____ WRITING: Details or Feelings

_3_ TOTAL   GRADE 1

Explanation:
The picture shows her fun day and has enough details for the beginning of the year. She sticks to the topic as she tells about driving the tractor but does not have enough text to get additional writing points.

Topic: My Fun Day

Writing Sample

Andrew
Me and dad we will go to the foltBoll feld. And fly A Donosor.
Wen the are not Playing fotboll. It will be fun. On a winde day
uv cos. I can not wet I til we do it. I am VAry happy I can not
wAt.

The Simple 6 ™ Mini Rubric

0 / 1

_1_	DRAWING:	Stick to the Topic
___	DRAWING:	Details
_1_	WRITING:	Stick to the Topic
_1_	WRITING:	Logical Order
___	WRITING:	Sentence Patterns
_1_	WRITING:	Details or Feelings
_4_	TOTAL	GRADE 1

Explanation:
This boy has quite a lot to say about flying what appears to be a dinosaur kite. Because I can't really tell what it is and the people are sticks, he gets a point for sticking to the topic, but not details. Writing points are given for sticking to the topic, having a beginning, middle, and end, and also for including details and feelings.

Topic: My Fun Day

Writing Sample

Mitchell
One day I went to the pottowataomi zoo! I went with my family to It. We saw African lions! we saw fritening bats to. then we saw froshus Alligaters! Then we went home.

The Simple 6 ™ Mini Rubric

0 / 1
_1_ DRAWING: Stick to the Topic
___ DRAWING: Details
_1_ WRITING: Stick to the Topic
_1_ WRITING: Logical Order
_1_ WRITING: Sentence Patterns
_1_ WRITING: Details or Feelings

_5_ TOTAL   GRADE 1

Explanation:
   Great story, with outstanding vocabulary words for a baseline sample! Work on drawing skills for the Score 6.

Topic: My Fun Day

Writing Sample

Kyle
My best day was when I played with my pitchingmachien. I expeshally liked to catch the popflys. First I wate intil my dad terns it on. If I hit a ball I will watch it go up. It's so fun!

The Simple 6 ™ Mini Rubric

0 / 1

_1_	DRAWING:	Stick to the Topic
_1_	DRAWING:	Details
_1_	WRITING:	Stick to the Topic
_1_	WRITING:	Logical Order
_1_	WRITING:	Sentence Patterns
_1_	WRITING:	Details or Feelings
_6_	TOTAL	GRADE 1

Explanation:
The picture shows the pitching machine in action, but I would encourage this student to include hands, feet, ears, and hair. The story covers all components.

Increase Expectations for Second Semester

The following student samples suggest expectations for scoring as the year progresses. Again, it is important to determine your own expectations as you articulate writing goals for K-2 with your colleagues.

TOPIC: My Fun Day

SECOND SEMESTER
Grade 1
Student Sample
Kevin

Score 1

Writing Sample

I Play with My Dad. My Dad Loves me.

The **Simple 6** ™ **Mini Rubric**

0 / 1

___	DRAWING:	Stick to the Topic
___	DRAWING:	Details
___	WRITING:	Stick to the Topic
___	WRITING:	Logical Order
___	WRITING:	Sentence Patterns
_1_	WRITING:	Details or Feelings
_1_	TOTAL	GRADE 1

Explanation:
 Since I cannot tell that the picture is of the boy and his dad playing, there is no point given for drawing. The short sentences give details but don't necessarily stick to the topic.

Topic: My Fun Day

Writing Sample

John
I like Easter because you get alos and alos candy

The Simple 6 ™ Mini Rubric

0 / 1

_1_	DRAWING:	Stick to the Topic
___	DRAWING:	Details
_1_	WRITING:	Stick to the Topic
___	WRITING:	Logical Order
___	WRITING:	Sentence Patterns
___	WRITING:	Details or Feelings
_2_	TOTAL	GRADE 1

Explanation:
    We assume that he has candy in his mouth and give one point for sticking to the topic in the drawing. He also attempts to stick to the topic in the writing, although he does not use the word fun.

Topic: My Fun Day

Writing Sample

Marlene
I had a picnick last summer. I was by myself Because
I had good stuff to eat.

The Simple 6 ™ Mini Rubric

0 / 1		
_1_	DRAWING:	Stick to the Topic
_1_	DRAWING:	Details
_1_	WRITING:	Stick to the Topic
____	WRITING:	Logical Order
____	WRITING:	Sentence Patterns
____	WRITING:	Details or Feelings
_3_	TOTAL	GRADE 1

Explanation:
    Notice how we get more and more details as students progress through Grade 1. Neatness improves as small muscles get better control. The story gets a point for sticking to the topic, even though the word fun is not mentioned. Details are there, but they do not contribute to the clarity of the story.

Topic: My Fun Day

Writing Sample

Sharon
The people having fun are my mom and I. We are reating a book. It's sunny outsaid. It's fun outsaid. There is a tree out-said and words outsaid. I like it.

The Simple 6 ™ Mini Rubric

0 / 1

_1_	DRAWING:	Stick to the Topic
___	DRAWING:	Details
_1_	WRITING:	Stick to the Topic
_1_	WRITING:	Logical Order
___	WRITING:	Sentence Patterns
_1_	WRITING:	Details or Feelings
_4_	TOTAL	GRADE 1

Explanation:
    The stick people kept her from getting 2 points on the drawing. Her story sticks to the topic, has order, and includes some details – even though it doesn't flow well.

Topic: My Fun Day

Writing Sample

Micah
My best day was When I went to see My Grandma and
Grandpa's House! We Go to a fantsy Hotel to swim. We go
too a video store and get movies. We play Games. We go on
bike rides. We get McDonald's. I like going there to vizit in
the summer!

The Simple 6 ™ **Mini Rubric**

0 / 1

_1_ DRAWING: Stick to the Topic
____ DRAWING: Details
_1_ WRITING: Stick to the Topic
_1_ WRITING: Logical Order
_1_ WRITING: Sentence Patterns
_1_ WRITING: Details or Feelings

_5_ TOTAL   GRADE 1

Explanation:
    This is a great story with lots of details.
By year end, I would like to see more details in the picture. If he's trying to avoid
drawing people, he could have drawn a face
in the window or a car driving up. When you
get in the Score 5 range, you always have to
ask yourself what is missing that would have
made it a definite Score 6.

120

© Pieces of Learning

Topic: My Fun Day

Writing Sample

Mike
My best day was when I scored a goal at my soccer game.
I played Bremen with my teammates. I felt marvalus!
Gremen is green. We are yellow. They probly felt very sad
but our team was happy. It was very very fun!

The Simple 6 ™ Mini Rubric

0 / 1

_1_ DRAWING: Stick to the Topic
_1_ DRAWING: Details
_1_ WRITING: Stick to the Topic
_1_ WRITING: Logical Order
_1_ WRITING: Sentence Patterns
_1_ WRITING: Details or Feelings

_6_ TOTAL   GRADE 1

Explanation:
   Great details and enthusiasm
all around. This is a strong Score 6
for the end of the year in Grade 1.

Assessment in Grade 2

Students entering Grade 2 always seem to make up an eclectic group. Ability levels range from students who are still struggling to read and write to those students who are fluently reading chapter books and writing multiple-paragraph stories. Grade 2 is a transition year. Remember, the first semester goal is to achieve a Score 6 on the writing/ drawing assessment. The second semester goal, however, is in line with the expectations for standardized assessment without drawing.

Suggested Expectations for Beginning Grade 2
Baseline Writing/Drawing Samples

Score 6	picture has many details	Sticks to the topic, has logical order, different sentence patterns, and includes many details/feelings
Score 5	picture has many details	Sticks to the topic, has logical order, different sentence patterns Or includes many details and/or feelings
Score 4	picture may have details	Sticks to the topic has logical order, and probably includes details/feelings
Score 3	picture may have details	Sticks to the topic, has logical order, OR details/feelings
Score 2	recognizable picture	Sticks to the topic
Score 1	attempts picture	OR attempts to stick to the topic

On the next page is an example of a prompt you might use for your baseline writing sample. It uses the Grade 1-2 mini rubric on page 71. When completed, it should be attached to the student sample. The prompt is followed by a set of anchor papers to help guide scoring.

Prompt: Being a Good Friend

Being a Good Friend

Friends are everywhere! They might live in your neighborhood. They might be in your class. Who are your friends? Why did you choose them for your friends?

Draw a picture and write a story about your friends. Be sure to show exactly what your friends look like, and tell why you chose them as friends.

On the next page, write a story about your friends.

TOPIC: Being A Good Friend

Writing Sample

Chris
My friend is Ben. I aLLways pLay with Ben.

The Simple 6 ™ Mini Rubric

0 / 1

___	DRAWING:	Stick to the Topic
___	DRAWING:	Details
_1_	WRITING:	Stick to the Topic
___	WRITING:	Logical Order
___	WRITING:	Sentence Patterns
___	WRITING:	Details or Feelings
_1_	TOTAL	GRADE 2

Explanation:
No credit is given for people without bodies in Grade 2. One point is given for sticking to the topic in the writing sample. This is a time when I might consider giving a half a point for sticking to the topic in the drawing and the writing.

TOPIC: Being A Good Friend

Writing Sample

Grant
How wold I be woth outno frands. ILL be LOLe I a m Luky tat
ean apon. my frends are ALek Brett Peter. Tay are nes
vonale.

The Simple 6 ™ Mini Rubric

0 / 1

_1_	DRAWING:	Stick to the Topic
___	DRAWING:	Details
_1_	WRITING:	Stick to the Topic
___	WRITING:	Logical Order
___	WRITING:	Sentence Patterns
___	WRITING:	Details or Feelings

_2_   TOTAL   GRADE 2

Explanation:
   I would score this paper one of two ways.
I would either give one point for the drawing and one point for the writing OR I would
give no point for drawing since there are no
hands or feet, and I would give points in
writing for sticking to the topic and attempting details — even though it's a real struggle
to understand what he's trying to say. Either
way, it's a Score 2.

TOPIC: Being A Good Friend

Writing Sample

Kevin
Brison is my friend becos I naw hem sinch I was a baby and
weyo be came bast frins I lik hem a lot

The Simple 6 ™ Mini Rubric

0 / 1
_1_ DRAWING: Stick to the Topic
___ DRAWING: Details
_1_ WRITING: Stick to the Topic
___ WRITING: Logical Order
___ WRITING: Sentence Patterns
_1_ WRITING: Details or Feelings

_3_ TOTAL   GRADE 2

Explanation:
This is a weak Score 3, but get points for sticking to the topic in the drawing and the writing, as well as giving details or feelings.

TOPIC: Being A Good Friend

Writing Sample

Ashley
I have 3 best friends. There names are Natalie, Delaney, Shelbi not counting me thow because that would make 4. I'm not own of them because I'm not my friend. I meet shelbi in kindergrden. I meet Delaney on the bus. I meet Natalie in 1st grade.

The **Simple6** ™ **Mini Rubric**

0 / 1
_1_ DRAWING: Stick to the Topic
_1_ DRAWING: Details
_1_ WRITING: Stick to the Topic
___ WRITING: Logical Order
___ WRITING: Sentence Patterns
_1_ WRITING: Details or Feelings

_4_ TOTAL   GRADE 2

Explanation:
    This is more the quality of drawing that should be expected by Grade 2, even though these girls don't have feet. Points are given for topic and details in the drawing, as well as topic and details in the writing. A conclusion would have given another point in logical order.

TOPIC: Being A Good Friend

Writing Sample

Nathan
My friends are Carson, Ben, Brant, Kevin, and Bryson. I've known Carson since preschool. I've known everybody else exepet Bryson and Kiven since 1st grade. I go over to Kiven's, Bryson's, and Carson's. I have lots of fun. I chose my friends because they are all nice. I like my friends.

The **Simple6** ™ **Mini Rubric**

0 / 1

_1_	DRAWING:	Stick to the Topic
_1_	DRAWING:	Details
_1_	WRITING:	Stick to the Topic
_1_	WRITING:	Logical Order
___	WRITING:	Sentence Patterns
_1_	WRITING:	Details or Feelings
_5_	TOTAL	GRADE 2

Explanation:
Friends in the drawing "have all their parts," including detailed faces, clothing, and name labels. The writing is well done, sticking to the topic, having order, and providing us with plenty of details. This is a great story that only needs to have sentence patterns that contribute to the overall fluency.

TOPIC: Being A Good Friend

Writing Sample

Meg
How would I ever be happy without my friends? My friends come to visit me at my house. I live on the cul da sack in our neighborhood. My friends aer Megan, Hannah, and Kristen. I know them because they live close by and because I am with them in girl scouts. I play with them at reces. I chose them because they care about me. They are also kind and generus. They always help me feel better. So that is how I got my friends. I like them all soooo much!

The Simple 6 ™ Mini Rubric
0 / 1
_1_   DRAWING: Stick to the Topic
_1_   DRAWING: Details
_1_   WRITING: Stick to the Topic
_1_   WRITING: Logical Order
_1_   WRITING: Sentence Patterns
_1_   WRITING: Details or Feelings

_6_   TOTAL   GRADE 2

Explanation:
    Points in all categories. Very well structured, also giving us details, feelings, different sentence patterns, and challenging vocabulary.

Moving into Formal Assessment
During the Second Semester

Whether your state starts formal assessment at Grade 3 or Grade 4, students are ready to start moving toward expectations for standardized testing. As soon as they are ready, begin the nine-week implementation of The Simple 6™ writing program. Details for implementation are in the next chapter. At the end of the chapter, you will see the second semester assessment packet and anchor papers that have been scored without drawing.

The Simple 6 ™

Stick to the Topic
Logical Order
Interesting Words
Different Sentence Patterns
Descriptive Sentences
Audience

Chapter 4: The Simple 6™: A Writing Rubric for Kids

What is The Simple 6™?

Review of the Components

The Rubric

Implementing The Simple 6™

   Writing Program

Nine Week Overview

The Simple 6™ Quick Reference Chart

Mini Rubrics

Class Analysis Chart

Quarterly Assessment Packet

Prompt and Anchor Papers

Quarterly Tracking Chart

Yearly Class Record

Chapter 4: The Simple 6 ™

A Writing Rubric for Kids

What is The Simple 6™?

The Simple 6™ is a student-friendly, simple analytic rubric. Originating in Indiana, its straightforward design meets academic standards and guides students during standardized writing assessments. Because there is no single, national standard for exemplary writing, each state has the jurisdiction to assess and evaluate independently. Most states offer a complex holistic rubric as their assessment tool, complete with phrases, questions, or narratives that define each point value. Each segment of the rubric has a phrase, a question, or a narrative that defines the point value. Assessment rubrics usually range from four to six points, including conventions or not. Some states add the points from two individual scorers or place the point value into a mathematical equation that will eventually become a total language arts score.

Scoring student writing with a complex holistic rubric is difficult. Why? Teachers give these reasons: *The language is too ambiguous. It's too difficult to understand exactly how to move from one level to the next. Scoring takes too much time. Choosing the line in the rubric that "best fits" doesn't always give a true assessment. I don't get it, so I just guess at the score, hoping to get close...* So what is really accomplished by asking teachers to use complex holistic rubrics with which they don't feel comfortable?

Rubrics are designed for two purposes: to assess and/or to articulate expectations. However, the term *rubric* is so often tied to assessment that teachers often forget to use a rubric to guide expectations. Asking myself the question, "What components of exemplary writing are seen in student writing samples that pass standardized assessments?" was really the key to developing The Simple 6™. My main focus, however, was never to just "beat the test." Knowing and learning to focus on the components of exemplary writing made my students outstanding writers.

Why does it work?

The Simple 6™ works because students as young as age seven *understand* it. The language is clear, the order is developmentally progressive, and the scoring is relatively uncomplicated. Each component builds on the next, allowing students to master skills as they cumulatively review and work together to take control of their own writing. Regardless of the state, these elements of exemplary writing are in *your* state scoring rubric.

Stick to the topic.
Check for logical order.
Include interesting words.
Use different sentence patterns
Write descriptive sentences.
Write for an audience.

Review of the Components for Students in Grades 2-5

Just Simple 6™ It!

Stick to the Topic

Did I stick to the topic and not run away with other ideas?

Did I answer or address all the questions in the prompt?

If there were no questions, did I design my own questions?

Logical Order

Is there an introduction, or did I just dive right in?

Did I use a lead or hook to get my readers interested?

Is my conclusion strong? Is it more than one sentence?

Is the body organized, probably by the questions in the prompt?

Did each paragraph address a new question?

Interesting Words/Challenging Vocabulary

Did I eliminate overused words such as *went, said, big, little,* and *good*?

Did I go back and look for three more opportunities to use challenging vocabulary?

Are my new words used correctly?

Different Sentence Patterns

Does my essay or story sound like a list?

Did I vary my sentence patterns, using questions, exclamations, and items in a series?

Did I write compound and/or complex sentences?

How many sentences start with prepositional, adverbial, or participial phrases?

Do my sentences have smooth transitions?

Descriptive Sentences

Did I create a vision for the reader that matches what I see in my head?

Did I use precise verbs?

Did I name people, places, and things with proper nouns?

Did I include adjectives – but not too many?

Did I appeal to the reader's senses?

Did I give several detailed examples?

Audience

Did I write for a specific audience?

Does my personality shine through my writing?

Does my tone match the prompt?

The following page is designed to be used as an assessment sheet for teachers or a guide as students write their rough drafts.

Name _____ Date _____

Title _____

The  Simple 6 ™ A Writing Rubric for Kids

Stick to the topic.
Check for logical order.
Include interesting words.
Use different sentence patterns.
Create descriptive sentences.
Write for an audience.

Ask these questions:

yes/no

_____ Did you **stick to the topic**, or did you run away with some other idea?

_____ Have you presented your thoughts in a **logical order** that included an inviting beginning and a strong conclusion?

_____ Have you gone back to look for opportunities to use **interesting words**?

_____ Did you use **different sentence patterns**, or does your story sound like a list?

_____ Does each paragraph have a topic sentence and supporting detail **sentences that are descriptive**?

_____ Did you write for an **audience**?
(original, lively, or another unique perspective appropriate for the prompt)

_____ **TOTAL POINTS** (How many did you answer YES?)

Implementing The Simple 6™ Writing Program

Step 1. Collect baseline data before you begin.

What writing skills do your students currently have? Make copies of the writing samples and put them in a separate folder that you may refer to throughout the year. At the end of the year, return these copies with their final writing samples. This is the easiest and truest documentation of growth.

Step 2. Make student folders.

Make a folder for each student. (A template can be found on p. 38 in <u>Writing: The Simple 6™</u>.) All the Thursday/Friday prompt writing will be kept in this folder. Use a sheet on the front to track writing topics and their dates. (If students are truly writing about what you're doing in class, you should be able to see the highlights of your curriculum by reviewing writing topics.)

Step 3. Use the "paper strategy" to organize writing time.

Students typically have a difficult time writing for 40 minutes or more. By helping them to manage each stage of writing, they use the time more wisely. In doing so, they write more thoroughly.

```
PLAN A
Brainstorming            7 minutes
Organizing Ideas         8 minutes
Rough Draft             15 minutes
REST OVER NIGHT
Revising/Editing        10 minutes
Final Draft             20 minutes
```

```
PLAN B
Prompt Attack           15 minutes
Rough Draft             15 minutes
REST OVER NIGHT
Revising/Editing        10 minutes
Final Draft             20 minutes
```

The Thursday/Friday teaching format is 60 minutes a day for nine weeks. Each 60-minute block is designed to include a lesson or motivation of some type, student interaction, and writing. Detailed descriptions for the actual teaching of The Simple 6™ can be found in Chapter 3 of <u>Writing: The Simple 6™</u>. This chapter includes a Thursday/Friday narrative, four follow-up activities, and standardized lesson plans for the narratives.

Nine Week Overview

Week 1: Stick to the Topic

Instructional Focus: Write about the assigned topic only.
Eliminate sentences that don't belong.
Use the prompt questions to guide the body.

Week 2: Logical Order

Instructional Focus: Retell well-known or familiar stories.
Create "human sentences."
Discuss transitional words and prepositional phrases.
Define expectations for an inviting introduction and a strong conclusion.

Week 3: Interesting Words

Instructional Focus: Replace generic vocabulary with at least three challenging words.
Eliminate *went* and *said*.

Week 4: Review, Share, and Revise

Instructional Focus: Review the elements of. . . sticking to the topic
logical order
interesting words
Think aloud as you model the writing process.
Vary instructional strategies.
Let students write in small groups.
Get all students to a Score 3.

Week 5: Different Sentence Patterns

Instructional Focus: List several sentences about the same topic.
Show variety by . . . changing word order
including questions
adding dialogue
inserting exclamations
adding prepositional phrases

Week 6: Descriptive Sentences

Instructional Focus: Introduce strategies, such as inserting . . .
- precise verbs
- proper nouns
- adjectives
- imagery
- literary devices

Week 7: Audience

Instructional Focus: Analyze commercials to get students thinking about how to communicate with an audience.
Write advice column responses.
Talk about how adjusting tone helps to connect with an audience.

Week 8: Peer Editing and Scoring

Instructional Focus: Show the entire *Simple 6™* rubric.
For each part of the process done well, one point will be given.
Practice scoring.

Week 9: Creating a Score 6

Instructional Focus: Share samples of Score 6 exemplary writing.
Review the steps for revision.
Give students an opportunity to work together or alone to create a passing paper.
Use several formats for revision.

Detailed lesson plans for the implementation of The Simple 6™ writing program are found in <u>Writing: The Simple 6™</u>. Chapter 3, p. 38.

Tips for Success: Stay FOCUSED!! Use the DATA!!

1. Stay on a Thursday/Friday schedule. Keep the same time each day.

2. Establish a place for the writing folders.

3. Make sure students document writing tasks each week and keep samples in their folders.

4. Pay particular attention during informal observation. Is everyone participating?

5. Analyze the data each week.

6. Identify weaknesses by rubric component or individual student.

7. Conference with flexible skill groups and/or individuals weekly.

8. Praise students for their progress every step of the way.

9. Approach each lesson with enthusiasm and encouragement.

10. Step aside and let students take charge of the reviews and discussions.

11. Post a *Simple 6*™ chart in your classroom, and refer to it every time students write.

12. Display writing samples, and encourage students to share ideas with one another.

13. Continue to use picture books to motivate students to write.

14. Plan for an art integration on Thursday afternoon so you can continue to reinforce the importance of drawing details that will enhance the writing.

Using The Simple 6™ to Guide and Assess Writing-only Prompts

While the primary focus of The Simple 6™ is to guide students as they write, it is also an invaluable assessment tool. The following pages are provided to simplify the assessment and documentation process.

The Simple 6™ Quick Reference Guide (page 143)

Use this sheet as a one-page reminder of The Simple 6™ components and their sub-topics. Make a copy for each student, and glue it to the inside of the writing folder. It is also helpful as a "cheat sheet" during student review.

The Simple 6™ Mini Rubric (page 144)

Designed to be cut into four pieces; attach a mini rubric to each student writing sample that will be assessed. Also, make them readily available for student use.

Class Analysis Chart (page 145)

As you complete each mini rubric, transfer the data onto the Class Analysis Chart. Use it to analyze current data and to drive future classroom instruction.

Formal Quarterly Assessment Packet (pages 146-149)

Designed to be printed in booklet format on 11" x 17" paper, this closely resembles the actual standardized testing format. Many administrators believe that if it looks like the "real thing," students will try harder and do better. Directly following the assessment packet are scored samples of student writing samples.

Quarterly Tracking Chart for your Current Class (page 156)

Use this chart to track the success of your teaching strategies each quarter. Check to make sure the percent of passing students increases each quarter. Local and standardized data may be combined on this chart for a true look at the entire year. This is also a great sheet for tracking data quarter by quarter for a school improvement plan.

Yearly Student Tracking Chart (page 157)

Designed for year-end data collection, this sheet clearly illustrates growth for individual students within a class. Five writing scores are displayed for each student. This chart should be turned in as documentation for a school improvement plan as well as being forwarded to the next year's teacher(s).

The Simple 6 ™

Quick Reference Chart for Elementary

Stick to the Topic

- Stick to the topic, and don't run away with other ideas.

- Follow the prompt instructions.

Logical Order

- BME (Beginning, Middle, End)

- Focus on the strong conclusion.

- Use the prompt to guide structure.

Interesting Words

- Include 3 challenging vocabulary attempts. (minimum)

- Eliminate generic words like *went* and *said*.

Varied Sentence Patterns

- Include questions, exclamations, and series.
- Focus on compound/complex sentences.
- Use direct quotations if appropriate.

Descriptive Sentences

- Use precise verbs.
- Include proper nouns.
- Insert adjectives
- Appeal to the reader's senses.

Audience

- Write in a tone that is appropriate for the prompt.
- Let your personality shine! (exclamations, thoughts, questions, humor, satire)

The Simple 6 ™

0 / 1

___ Stick to the Topic
___ Logical Order
___ Interesting Words
___ Different Sentence Patterns
___ Descriptive Sentences
___ Audience
___ TOTAL POINTS

©Kay Davidson, Revised 2002

The Simple 6 ™

0 / 1

___ Stick to the Topic
___ Logical Order
___ Interesting Words
___ Different Sentence Patterns
___ Descriptive Sentences
___ Audience
___ TOTAL POINTS

©Kay Davidson, Revised 2002

The Simple 6 ™

0 / 1

___ Stick to the Topic
___ Logical Order
___ Interesting Words
___ Different Sentence Patterns
___ Descriptive Sentences
___ Audience
___ TOTAL POINTS

©Kay Davidson, Revised 2002

The Simple 6 ™

0 / 1

___ Stick to the Topic
___ Logical Order
___ Interesting Words
___ Different Sentence Patterns
___ Descriptive Sentences
___ Audience
___ TOTAL POINTS

©Kay Davidson, Revised 2002

The Simple 6™ Class Analysis Chart

Prompt _____ Date _____

NAMES	Stick to the Topic	Logical Order	Interesting Words	Sentence Patterns	Descriptive Sentences	Audience	TOTAL

Comments

Student _____ Assessment Packet
Teacher _____ Grade 2 -5
Date _____

SCORE ___/6
___/4

Title

Read the information in the box. Then do the writing activity.

Prompt scenario. Questions.

Directions. Repeat the questions in sentence format.

Pre-Writing Activity

Plan your writing on another sheet of paper before you begin.
Be sure your story has a beginning, a middle, and an end.
Here are some questions to help you think about your story.
* *
* *
* *

Include as many details as you can to make your writing interesting.

_____

_____

_____

_____

_____

_____

_____

_____

_____

_____

_____

_____

_____

_____

_____

_____

_____

_____

_____

_____

_____

_____

_____

_____

_____

_____

_____

_____

_____

_____

_____

_____

_____

_____

Your writing will be scored on how well you get your ideas across. Be sure to check everything over before you turn in your story.

Proofreading Checklist

1. Have you capitalized names and sentence beginnings?
2. Have you ended each sentence with the correct punctuation mark?
3. Have you checked for spelling mistakes?
4. Did you write complete sentences?

The Simple 6™ A Writing Rubric for Kids

CONTENT RUBRIC

Ask these questions:

0 / 1

____ **STICK TO THE TOPIC:** Did you **stick to the topic**, or did you run away with some other idea?

____ **LOGICAL ORDER:** Have you presented your thoughts in a **logical order** that included an inviting beginning and a strong conclusion?

____ **INTERESTING WORDS:** Have you overused generic vocabulary, or have you gone back to look for opportunities to use **interesting words?**

____ **DIFFERENT SENTENCE PATTERNS:** Have you tried to create interest and variety by using **different sentence patterns?**

____ **DESCRIPTIVE SENTENCES:** Did you write **descriptive sentences** that made the reader aware of his senses?

____ **AUDIENCE:** Did you write for a specific **audience?** Were you original, lively, or authoritative?

© Kay Davidson, 2004

____ / 6 TOTAL POINTS

LANGUAGE CONVENTIONS RUBRIC

☐ SCORE 4 VERY GOOD	☐ SCORE 3 ADEQUATE	☐ SCORE 2 MINIMAL	☐ SCORE 1 POOR
• There are few or no errors in: capitalization punctuation subj./verb agreement complete sentences spelling	• There are some errors in: capitalization punctuation subj./verb agreement complete sentences spelling	• There are many errors in: capitalization punctuation subj./verb agreement complete sentences spelling	• There are many serious errors in: capitalization punctuation subj./verb agreement complete sentences spelling

Student Samples for Formal Assessment

Prompt: Show and Tell

Your class is having Show and Tell this Friday. On Show and Tell Day, you get to bring something from home and tell your friends about it. Draw a picture, and write a story that tells what you will bring for Show and Tell. What will you bring? What will you say about it? What will your friends think?

Grade 2 Second Semester

The following student samples are scored using The Simple 6™: A Writing Rubric for Kids

TOPIC: Show and Tell   Kenny: Grade 2 Score 1

My Dog

What is it's name?
This Dog is tring.

Rubric Assessment:

The **Simple 6** ™
A Writing Rubric for Kids

0 / 1

att. 1   Stick to the Topic
____   Logical Order
____   Interesting Words
____   Different Sentence Patterns
____   Descriptive Sentences
____   Audience

_1_   TOTAL POINTS

Assessment Commentary:
A Score 1 paper is short. It is hard to make sense of it as you are reading. This paper, which seems to be about Show and Tell, is lacking in content and hard to follow. The student has attempted to stick to the topic because we assume the dog will be brought in for Show and Tell. One point is given for attempting to stick to the topic. In papers that will not pass, points are usually given for attempts so the student is encouraged to do better the next time. Try to avoid giving students 0 points when they have tried.

my Sling Shout

I will show them how to shout it and then I will show them how to hold it then I will show them how to ame it

Rubric Assessment:

The Simple 6 ™

A Writing Rubric for Kids

0 / 1
att. 1 Stick to the Topic
att. 1 Logical Order
____ Interesting Words
____ Different Sentence Patterns
____ Descriptive Sentences
____ Audience

_2_ TOTAL POINTS

Assessment Commentary:
A Score 2 paper is relatively short, but it is usually longer than a Score 1 paper. This paper, which seems to be about Show and Tell, but never really mentions the words in the topic. Since we infer this, we give the point for attempting to stick to the topic. The student lists what he is going to do in a specific order. He gets the point for attempting logical order, even though there is no introduction or conclusion. No other points are given.

TOPIC: Show and Tell   Hannah: Grade 2 Score 3

My Frog

This is a frog. This frog come from a pond. He hop out on the bus and then he hop into the school. My frog is slimy. He is brown and green. He love to eat bugs. He fist bupy on him back. He is in the water. Now you know my Show and tell.

Rubric Assessment:

The Simple 6 ™

A Writing Rubric for Kids

0 / 1

_1_ Stick to the Topic
_1_ Logical Order
___ Interesting Words
___ Different Sentence Patterns
_1_ Descriptive Sentences
___ Audience

_3_ TOTAL POINTS

Assessment Commentary:
This paper gets 3 points. He sticks to the topic, even though Show and Tell is not mentioned until the end. He has an order in which he introduces his topic, tells about it, and ends the story. He gives many examples that describe the frog.

My Dog

Do you have a dog? I do and I'm going to bring him in for Show and Tell this week. He is the BEST! His name is Jason he is fun to play with. He is running around the classroom. Everyone is lafing. My grandma got it for me. He is a golden retriever. People love to pet it. He is Gigantic. He is Responsible to gard our house. He loves to catch a rackoon. He barks and his birthday is in April. I love him, don't you?

Rubric Assessment:

A Writing Rubric for Kids

0 / 1

_1_   Stick to the Topic

____   Logical Order

_1_   Interesting Words

____   Different Sentence Patterns

_1_   Descriptive Sentences

_1_   Audience

_4_   TOTAL POINTS

Assessment Commentary:
This is interesting with a great deal of potential. He sticks to the topic, but his ideas are scattered and make the body hard to follow. Interesting words for a second grader are retriever, gigantic, responsible, *and* guard. *Sentence patterns give this piece a choppy feel to it. Although there could be more details, he does have several descriptive sentences. He makes 2 direct connections to the audience.*

If I Had my Kitten

I got my kitten from my namber. The ketten was a boy. I named him Pomppcin. He was orange with wite stripes and was small, qoot, and fuzy. He liked to go under the gas tank and loved it win I holeded him and petted him to. Would you like a kitten like mine? Would you won't to biy him? Well he isn't for sell.

But if he was for sell he would't be here. Won stormy night the wind holed like wovs, the thunder crasht like a free fell, the lightning lit like the sun, the rane pored like a jug of milk poring in a cup.

Then the nexed day the sun shone so bright, and the grass so green but no orange wighte qott fuzy ketten. I never saw Popcin again! Have you lost somewon you loved? I did. If I still had my ketten I would bring him for Show and Tell.

Rubric Assessment:

The Simple 6 ™

A Writing Rubric for Kids
0 / 1
_1_ Stick to the Topic
_1_ Logical Order
____ Interesting Words
_1_ Different Sentence Patterns
_1_ Descriptive Sentences
_1_ Audience

_5_ TOTAL POINTS

Assessment Commentary:
The quality of the descriptive sentences is very impressive for a young writer. She sticks to the topic in a roundabout way, has order, but no challenging vocabulary. Different sentence patterns make the story flow. This young writer has unusual talent for using literary devices, and she pulls at your heartstrings as well. I would be letting this little girl know that she has talent as a writer!

The Amazing Secret!

My show and tell is going to be amazing! When I bring it in everybody is going to drool! I am going to tell everything about it and they will all love it, even the teacher!!! It's going to be so exiting! Even the Prindent of the United States of Amacia is going to love it so much they are going to give me a HUGE BANQUET! Everybody is going to love it! I am going to be absolootly thrilled! At the end of it I'm going to bring in the surprise and make all the kids jump so high! And you wanna know what it is going to be? It's an adoorable puppy!

Rubric Assessment: :

The Simple 6 ™

A Writing Rubric for Kids

0 / 1

_1_ Stick to the Topic

_1_ Logical Order

_1_ Interesting Words

_1_ Different Sentence Patterns

_1_ Descriptive Sentences

_1_ Audience

_6_ TOTAL POINTS

Assessment Commentary:
The connection with the audience jumps out at you right away. This is a very unusual style for a second grader in that she waits until the end to build up to the topic. Keeping you in suspense, she gives details about her Show and Tell, but she never gives details or clues about what it is. Interesting words (challenging vocabulary) were drool, banquet, absolutely, *and* adorable. *This is a well-written, unusual Score 6.*

Comparing Data for Your Current Class

Teacher: _____

Date _____ Task _____ % Passing _____ % Not Passing _____

	# of Students	Score 0 N %	Score 1 N %	Score 2 N %	Score 3 N %	Score 4 N %	Score 5 N %	Score 6 N %
(6) Writing Application								
(4) Lang. Conventions								

Date _____ Task _____ % Passing _____ % Not Passing _____

	# of Students	Score 0 N %	Score 1 N %	Score 2 N %	Score 3 N %	Score 4 N %	Score 5 N %	Score 6 N %
(6) Writing Application								
(4) Lang. Conventions								

Date _____ Task _____ % Passing _____ % Not Passing _____

	# of Students	Score 0 N %	Score 1 N %	Score 2 N %	Score 3 N %	Score 4 N %	Score 5 N %	Score 6 N %
(6) Writing Application								
(4) Lang. Conventions								

Date _____ Task _____ % Passing _____ % Not Passing _____

	# of Students	Score 0 N %	Score 1 N %	Score 2 N %	Score 3 N %	Score 4 N %	Score 5 N %	Score 6 N %
(6) Writing Application								
(4) Lang. Conventions								

Yearly Class Record

Year: _____ Teacher: _____

STUDENT NAMES	BASELINE:AUG. CONT (6) /CONV (4)	PROMPT 1:OCT. CONT (6)/CONV (4)	PROMPT 2: JAN. CONT (6) / CONV (4)	PROMPT 3:MAR. CONT (6) / CONV (4)	FINAL: MAY CONT (6)/CONV (4)
% PASSING APP./CONV.	/	/	/	/	/

Chapter 5:   Prompts for Beginning Writers

Kindergarten Assessment Packet
Prompts for Kindergarten Students

Grade 1 Assessment Packet
Prompts for Grade 1 Students

Grade 2 Assessment Packet
Prompts for Grade 2 Students
  1st Semester: with drawing
  2nd Semester: without drawing

Chapter 5: Prompts for Beginning Writers

Writing ideas have been given in previous chapters for making connections to picture books. They wouldn't necessarily be considered "prompts," and students don't always have to write to a full-blown prompt. We can get just as much (and sometimes more) from students by just introducing an idea, rather than bogging them down with questions that they have to answer as they write.

Why give young students a formal assessment anyway? Even though standardized testing may be years down the road, it is important to track student progress. Baseline and final writing samples show exactly how much writing progress was made throughout the year. Even one assessment at midyear will give a clear indication of how much progress is being made along the way. The purpose for periodic formative assessment is to increase student achievement by looking at the data and adjusting instruction accordingly.

Thinking within the Social Hierarchy

Prompt samples are everywhere. There are several books available that are filled with prompts and prompt ideas, and there are numerous web sites that list prompts and ideas as well. Many schools, however, design their own prompts so they are written in a style that closely simulates their state assessment. As you think about developing prompts that are appropriate for elementary students, consider working within the social hierarchy. Here is a framework to consider as you design prompts for elementary students.

Kindergarten: Me, My Family

Grade 1:   Me, My Family, My Friends
Grade 2:   Me, My Friends, My Neighborhood, My School
Grade 3:   Me, My School, My Community
Grade 4:   My School, My Community, My State
Grade 5:   My Friends, My State or Region, My Country
Grade 6:   My Country, My World

The data derived during these assessments identifies student strengths and weaknesses, as well as their entry and exit levels of writing ability. This information is then readily available to guide classroom instruction. It should also be used as documentation for a school improvement plan. The prompts provided in this chapter are designed to be page 1 of the four-page quarterly assessment packet that is shown on the following pages.

Student _____

Teacher _____

Date _____

SCORE ___/6

___/4

Title

Listen to the directions. Then do the drawing and writing activity.

Pre-Drawing and Pre-Writing Activity

Here are some questions to help with your drawing and writing:

Be sure to include details to make your drawing and writing interesting.

Your drawing and writing will be scored on how well you get your ideas across. Be sure to check everything over before you turn it in.

Draw a Picture.

Write a story.

A Rubric for Beginning Writers
Kindergarten

CONTENT RUBRIC

Ask these questions:

0 / 1

DRAWING:

____ Did you **stick to the topic** in your drawing?

____ Are the main elements in your drawing **recognizable**?

____ Does your picture show **details** or a **background**?

WRITING:

____ Did you **stick to the topic** in your writing?

____ Have you written your thoughts in an **order** that makes sense?

____ Did you **describe** or tell about your **feelings**?

____ / 6 **TOTAL POINTS** How many did you answer YES?

© Kay Davidson, 2005

LANGUAGE CONVENTIONS RUBRIC

☐ SCORE 4 VERY GOOD	☐ SCORE 3 ADEQUATE	☐ SCORE 2 MINIMAL	☐ SCORE 1 LESS THAN MINIMAL
• **More than one sentence with few/no errors in:** capitalization end marks spelling of high-frequency words	• **One sentence that may have errors in:** capitalization end marks spelling of high-frequency words	• **A partial sentence that may have errors in:** capitalization end marks spelling of high-frequency words	• **A word or less that contains:** no letters or numbers scribble writing no spaces no punctuation
left-right progression spaces between words invented spelling	left-right progression spaces between words invented spelling	left-right progression spaces between words invented spelling	

Prompts for Kindergarten Students
Focus: Me/My Family

Prompts for Kindergarten students should be simple and to the point. They should have one focus, so students don't struggle with what to draw. Additionally, when asking students to draw and write, there should not be a conflict between the tasks. An example of this would be:

PROMPT A
I'm glad you're in my class! What is your name? What do you look like? What do you like to do?

In this prompt students would have a tendency to draw a portrait likeness of themselves until they think about showing what they like to do. Now their vision changes from a detailed, close-up portrait to a scene in the backyard, where they will immediately become a stick figure.

A better prompt would be:

PROMPT B
I'm glad you're in my class! What is your name? What do you look like? What makes you look different from everyone else in this class?

The prompts on the following pages have been designed with Kindergarten students in mind, but they can also be used for Grade one and early Grade two.

Prompt List for Kindergarten

I Like _____	I Do NOT Like _____
Today I Saw a _____	My Birthday
My Toy	My Family
My Mom	Me
What I Like to Do	My Friend
My Home	My Wish

Name _____ Date _____

I Like _____

Listen to the directions. Then do the drawing and writing activity.

Everybody has something they really like. It might be a place, a food, a toy, or even a person!

Draw a picture and write a story about something you really like.

Pre-Drawing and Pre-Writing Activity

Here is a question to help with your drawing and writing:
    What do you like?

Be sure to include details to make your drawing and writing interesting.

Your drawing and writing will be scored on how well you get your ideas across. Be sure to check everything over before you turn it in.

Name _____ Date _____

Today I Saw _____

Listen to the directions. Then do the drawing and writing activity.

Think of something you saw on your way to school today. Tell me about it. What did it look like? Why did you notice it?

Draw a picture and write a story about something you saw today.

Pre-Drawing and Pre-Writing Activity

Here are some questions to help with your drawing and writing:
    What did you see today?
    Why did you notice it?

Be sure to include details to make your drawing and writing interesting.

Your drawing and writing will be scored on how well you get your ideas across. Be sure to check everything over before you turn it in.

Name _____ Date _____

My Toy

Listen to the directions. Then do the drawing and writing activity.

Everyone has a toy or something they like to play with. What is your favorite toy? Why do you like it so much?

Draw a picture and write a story about your favorite toy.

Pre-Drawing and Pre-Writing Activity

Here are some questions to help with your drawing and writing:
    What is your favorite toy?
    Why do you like it so much?

Be sure to include details to make your drawing and writing interesting.

Your drawing and writing will be scored on how well you get your ideas across. Be sure to check everything over before you turn it in.

Name _____ Date _____

My Mom

Listen to the directions. Then do the drawing and writing activity.

Moms are special, and everyone's mom looks different! What does your mom look like? What makes her look different from other moms?

Draw a picture of your mom and tell what she looks like.

Pre-Drawing and Pre-Writing Activity

Here are some questions to help with your drawing and writing:

What does your mom look like?
What makes her look different from other moms?

Be sure to include details to make your drawing and writing interesting.

Your drawing and writing will be scored on how well you get your ideas across. Be sure to check everything over before you turn it in.

Name _____ Date _____

What I Like to Do

Listen to the directions. Then do the drawing and writing activity.

What do you like to do best? Do you like to do it alone or with someone?

Draw a picture showing you doing what you like to do best.

Pre-Drawing and Pre-Writing Activity

Here are some questions to help with your drawing and writing:

What do you like to do?
Do you like to do it by yourself?
Do you like to do it with someone?

Show yourself doing what you like to do best.
Be sure to include details to make your drawing and writing interesting.

Your drawing and writing will be scored on how well you get your ideas across. Be sure to check everything over before you turn it in.

My Home

Listen to the directions. Then do the drawing and writing activity.

Kids live in all different kinds of homes! Some are houses, and some are apartments. Some are big, and some are small. What does your home look like? What makes your home special to you?

Draw a picture of your home. Then write a story about what your home looks like and why it is special.

Pre-Drawing and Pre-Writing Activity

Here are some questions to help with your drawing and writing:

What does your home look like?
What makes your home special?

Be sure to include details to make your drawing and writing interesting.

Your drawing and writing will be scored on how well you get your ideas across. Be sure to check everything over before you turn it in.

Name _____ Date _____

I Do NOT Like _____

Listen to the directions. Then do the drawing and writing activity.

We like some things, and others we don't like. They might be books, TV shows, foods, certain kinds of clothes, or shoes. Is there something you really don't like? What is it?

Draw a picture of something you do not like. Tell why you feel this way.

Pre-Drawing and Pre-Writing Activity

Here are some questions to help with your drawing and writing:

Is there something you do not like?
Why do you feel this way?

Be sure to include details to make your drawing and writing interesting.

Your drawing and writing will be scored on how well you get your ideas across. Be sure to check everything over before you turn it in.

Name _____ Date _____

My Birthday

Listen to the directions. Then do the drawing and writing activity.

It is so exciting when our birthdays roll around. When is your birthday? Why do you like birthdays?

Draw a picture of something you did on your last birthday. Be sure to tell when your birthday is.

Pre-Drawing and Pre-Writing Activity

Here are some questions to help with your drawing and writing:

What did you do on your last birthday?
When is your birthday?

Be sure to include details to make your drawing and writing interesting.

Your drawing and writing will be scored on how well you get your ideas across. Be sure to check everything over before you turn it in.

Name _____ Date _____

My Family

Listen to the directions. Then do the drawing and writing activity.

Our families are the people we live with. Who is in your family? What do they look like?

Draw a picture of your family, and tell what each person looks like.

Pre-Drawing and Pre-Writing Activity

Here are some questions to help with your drawing and writing:

Who is in your family?
What do they look like?

Be sure to include details to make your drawing and writing interesting.

Your drawing and writing will be scored on how well you get your ideas across. Be sure to check everything over before you turn it in.

Me

Listen to the directions. Then do the drawing and writing activity.

I'm glad you are in my class! I want to know more about you! What do you look like? What do you like best about yourself?

Draw a picture that shows me what you look like. Write a story that tells what you like best about yourself.

Pre-Drawing and Pre-Writing Activity

Here are some questions to help with your drawing and writing:

What do you look like?
What do you like best about yourself?

Be sure to include details to make your drawing and writing interesting.

Your drawing and writing will be scored on how well you get your ideas across. Be sure to check everything over before you turn it in.

My Friend

Listen to the directions. Then do the drawing and writing activity.

Friends can be big or small, young or old. They can be people you meet at school, in your church, at your day care, or in your neighborhood.

Draw a picture of your friend. Tell why you like your friend.

Pre-Drawing and Pre-Writing Activity

Here are some questions to help with your drawing and writing:

Who is your friend?
Why do you like your friend?

Be sure to include details to make your drawing and writing interesting.

Your drawing and writing will be scored on how well you get your ideas across. Be sure to check everything over before you turn it in.

Name _____ Date _____

My Wish

Listen to the directions. Then do the drawing and writing activity.

One night you had a dream that a fairy gave you one magic wish. What did you wish for? Were you happy after the wish?

Draw a picture and write a story about what you wished for. Tell how you felt after your wish was granted.

Pre-Drawing and Pre-Writing Activity

Here are some questions to help with your drawing and writing:

What was your wish?
How did you feel after getting your wish?

Be sure to include details to make your drawing and writing interesting.

Your drawing and writing will be scored on how well you get your ideas across. Be sure to check everything over before you turn it in.

Student _____
Teacher _____
Date _____

Assessment Packet
Grade 1

SCORE ___/6
___/4

Title

Listen to the directions. Then do the drawing and writing activity.

Pre-Drawing and Pre-Writing Activity

Here are some questions to help with your drawing and writing:

Be sure to include details to make your drawing and writing interesting.

Your drawing and writing will be scored on how well you get your ideas across. Be sure to check everything over before you turn it in.

Draw a picture.

Write a story.

A Rubric for Beginning Writers
Grade 1

Ask these questions:

0 / 1

DRAWING:

____ Did you **stick to the topic** in your drawing?

____ Does your picture show **details** or a **background**?

WRITING:

____ Did you **stick to the topic** in your writing?

____ Have you written your thoughts in an **order** that makes sense?

____ Did you include **different sentence patterns**?

____ Did you **describe** or tell about your **feelings**?

____ / 6 TOTAL POINTS How many did you answer YES?

© Kay Davidson, 2005

LANGUAGE CONVENTIONS RUBRIC

☐ SCORE 4 VERY GOOD	☐ SCORE 3 ADEQUATE	☐ SCORE 2 MINIMAL	☐ SCORE 1 LESS THAN MINIMAL
• There are few or no errors in: capitalization punctuation subj./verb agreement complete sentences spelling	• There are some errors in: capitalization punctuation subj./verb agreement complete sentences spelling	• There are many errors in: capitalization punctuation subj./verb agreement complete sentences spelling	• There are many serious errors in: capitalization punctuation subj./verb agreement complete sentences spelling

Prompts for Students in Grade 1
Focus: Family/Home

Students in Grade 1 should now be focusing on the five-sentence paragraph. For some, this will be a struggle. Others will go far beyond this during the year. As students begin to develop stories, it is important that they learn about structure from the very beginning. There are basically two types of prompts:

3-Question Prompt
What is your story about?
What is the first event?
What is the second event?
What is the third event?
How does your story end?

What-Why Prompt
What did you choose?
Why #1
Why #2
Why #3
What are your feelings?

Prompt List for Grade 1
> My Family
> What I Like Best
> My Favorite Color
> My House
> My Good Friend
> My Teacher
> I Like to Play
> _____ with my Family
> All About Me
> Someone Special in my Family
> I Don't Like _____
> What I've Learned

Name _____ Date _____

My Family

Listen to the directions. Then do the drawing and writing activity.

Families come in all shapes and sizes. Who is in your family? What do they look like?

Draw a picture of your family that shows what each person looks like. Then write a story telling me all about your family.

Pre-Drawing and Pre-Writing Activity

Here are some questions to help with your drawing and writing:

Who is in your family?
What do they look like?

Be sure to include details to make your drawing and writing interesting.

Your drawing and writing will be scored on how well you get your ideas across. Be sure to check everything over before you turn it in.

What I Like Best

Listen to the directions. Then do the drawing and writing activity.

Your teacher is making a bulletin board showing the things that you and your friends like best. It might be something you have, something you like to eat, or something you like to play. What do you like best? Can you describe it in detail? Why do you like it?

Draw a picture of the thing you like best. Draw carefully, so I can easily tell what it is. On the next page, write a story about what you like best. Be sure to tell me why you like it.

Pre-Drawing and Pre-Writing Activity

Here are some questions to help with your drawing and writing:

What do you like best?
Why do you like it?

Be sure to include details to make your drawing and writing interesting.

Your drawing and writing will be scored on how well you get your ideas across. Be sure to check everything over before you turn it in.

Name _____   Date _____

My Favorite Color

Listen to the directions. Then do the drawing and writing activity.

Everyone in the class has been asked to choose their favorite color. What is your favorite color? Can you name some things that are this color? Why do you like it so much?

Draw a picture of something that is your favorite color. Write a story about your favorite color, and tell why you like it so much.

Pre-Drawing and Pre-Writing Activity

Here are some questions to help with your drawing and writing:

   What color do you like best?
   Can you name some things that are this color?
   Why do you like it?

Be sure to include details to make your drawing and writing interesting.

Your drawing and writing will be scored on how well you get your ideas across. Be sure to check everything over before you turn it in.

My House

Listen to the directions. Then do the drawing and writing activity.

Houses come in all shapes, sizes, and colors. What does your house look like? How can you tell it apart from the rest of the houses on your block?

Draw a picture, and write a story about your house. Include as many interesting details as you can.

Pre-Drawing and Pre-Writing Activity

Here are some questions to help with your drawing and writing:

What does your house look like?
How can you tell it apart from the others on your block?

Be sure to include details to make your drawing and writing interesting.

Your drawing and writing will be scored on how well you get your ideas across. Be sure to check everything over before you turn it in.

A Good Friend

Listen to the directions. Then do the drawing and writing activity.

We have many good friends throughout our lives. A good friend is someone that you like and someone you enjoy playing with. Who is your good friend? Why do you like this friend? What do you and your friend do together?

Draw a picture, and write a story about your good friend. Include as many interesting details as you can.

Pre-Drawing and Pre-Writing Activity

Here are some questions to help with your drawing and writing:

Who is your good friend?
Why do you like this friend?
What do you and your friend do together?

Be sure to include details to make your drawing and writing interesting.

Your drawing and writing will be scored on how well you get your ideas across. Be sure to check everything over before you turn it in.

My Teacher

Listen to the directions. Then do the drawing and writing activity.

Teachers spend many hours with their students each day. They try to make school fun while they teach you new things and keep you safe. Who is your teacher? How does your teacher make school fun?

Draw a picture, and write a story about your teacher doing something fun with the class.

Pre-Drawing and Pre-Writing Activity

Here are some questions to help with your drawing and writing:

Who is your teacher?
How does your teacher make school fun?

Be sure to include details to make your drawing and writing interesting.

Your drawing and writing will be scored on how well you get your ideas across. Be sure to check everything over before you turn it in.

I Like to Play

Listen to the directions. Then do the drawing and writing activity.

Playing is fun! Sometimes we like to play with our friends, and sometimes we just like to play alone. What do you like to do when you play?

Draw a picture, and write a story that tells all about what you like to do when you play.

Pre-Drawing and Pre-Writing Activity

Here are some questions to help with your drawing and writing:

    With whom do you play?
    What do like to do when you play?
    Why do you like it so much?

Be sure to include details to make your drawing and writing interesting.

Your drawing and writing will be scored on how well you get your ideas across. Be sure to check everything over before you turn it in.

Name _____ Date _____

_____ with My Family

Listen to the directions. Then do the drawing and writing activity.

Families are different, and they all like to do different things together. What do you like to do best with your family? Where do you do it? Tell all about it.

Draw a picture, and write a story about what you like to do with your family.

Pre-Drawing and Pre-Writing Activity

Here are some questions to help with your drawing and writing:

What do you like to do best with your family?
Where do you usually do it?

Be sure to include details to make your drawing and writing interesting.

Your drawing and writing will be scored on how clearly get your ideas across. Be sure to check everything over before you turn it in.

Name _____ Date _____

All About Me

Listen to the directions. Then do the drawing and writing activity.

I am glad you are in my first grade class. I want to know all about you. What is your full name? Do you have a nickname? What do you want me to know about you?

Draw a picture, and write a story about yourself. Include as many interesting details as you can.

Pre-Drawing and Pre-Writing Activity

Here are some questions to help with your drawing and writing:

    What is your name?
    Do you have a nickname?
    What do you want me to know about you?

Be sure to include details to make your drawing and writing interesting.

Your drawing and writing will be scored on how well you get your ideas across. Be sure to check everything over before you turn it in.

Name _____ Date _____

Someone Special in My Family

Listen to the directions. Then do the drawing and writing activity.

The people in your family are your mom, dad, brothers, sisters, aunts, uncles, cousins, and grandparents. Is there someone special in your family? What do you do with this person? What makes this person so special?

Draw a picture of you with someone special from your family. On the next page, write a story about this person. Be sure to tell me why this person is so special.

Pre-Drawing and Pre-Writing Activity

Here are some questions to help with your drawing and writing:

Who is a special person in your family?
What do you do with this person?
What makes this person so special?

Be sure to include details to make your drawing and writing interesting.

Your drawing and writing will be scored on how well you get your ideas across. Be sure to check everything over before you turn it in.

Name _____ Date _____

I Don't Like _____

Listen to the directions. Then do the drawing and writing activity.

There are some things in this world we just don't like. It may be a certain kind of food, a TV show, or a place you don't like to go. What is it that you don't like? Why don't you like it?

Draw a picture of something you don't like. On the next page, write a story about it, telling why you don't like it.

Pre-Drawing and Pre-Writing Activity

Here are some questions to help with your drawing and writing:

What is it that you don't like?
Why?

Be sure to include details to make your drawing and writing interesting.

Your drawing and writing will be scored on how well you get your ideas across. Be sure to check everything over before you turn it in.

Name _____ Date _____

What I've Learned

Listen to the directions. Then do the drawing and writing activity.

We come to school to learn. At the end of each year, we realize we have learned many new things. What did you learn this year? Think of just one new thing you learned. What is it? How do you feel about learning this new thing?

Draw a picture of yourself doing **one** of the things you learned this year. Write a story that tells all about it.

Pre-Drawing and Pre-Writing Activity

Here are some questions to help with your drawing and writing:

What did you learn this year?
How do you feel about it?

Be sure to include details to make your drawing and writing interesting.

Your drawing and writing will be scored on how well you get your ideas across. Be sure to check everything over before you turn it in.

Student _____

Teacher _____

Date _____

Assessment Packet
Beginning Grade 2

SCORE ____/6

____/4

Title

Read the information in the box. Then do the drawing and writing activity.

Prompt scenario. Questions.

Directions. Repeat the questions in sentence format.

Pre-Writing Activity

Plan your writing on another sheet of paper before you begin.
Be sure your story has a beginning, a middle, and an end.
Here are some questions to help you think about your story.

*

*

*

Include as many details as you can to make your writing interesting.

Draw a picture.

Write a story.

A Rubric for Beginning Writers
Early Grade 2

Ask these questions:

0 / 1

DRAWING:

____ Did you **stick to the topic** in your drawing?

____ Does your picture show **details** or a **background**?

WRITING:

____ Did you **stick to the topic** in your writing?

____ Have you written your thoughts in an **order** that makes sense?

____ Did you include **different sentence patterns**?

____ Did you **describe** or tell about your **feelings**?

____ / 6 TOTAL POINTS   How many did you answer YES?

© Kay Davidson, 2005

LANGUAGE CONVENTIONS RUBRIC

☐ SCORE 4 VERY GOOD	☐ SCORE 3 ADEQUATE	☐ SCORE 2 MINIMAL	☐ SCORE 1 LESS THAN MINIMAL
• There are few or no errors in: capitalization punctuation subj./verb agreement complete sentences spelling	• There are some errors in: capitalization punctuation subj./verb agreement complete sentences spelling	• There are many errors in: capitalization punctuation subj./verb agreement complete sentences spelling	• There are many serious errors in: capitalization punctuation subj./verb agreement complete sentences spelling

Prompts for Students in Grade 2
Focus: Me/My Friends/My Neighborhood/My School

Students in Grade 2 or 3 may be considered "transition writers," depending on when your state's formal assessment is given. Even in those states where formal assessment isn't given until Grade 4, students in Grade 2 have the cognitive ability to write complex stories that are built within a structure. Because of the developmental differences in Grade 2 students, following are writing/drawing prompts for the first semester and writing-only prompts for the second semester. Again, focus on structure.

3 Question Prompt	What-Why Prompt
What is your story about?	What did you choose?
1st Event – Detail	Why #1 – Detail
2nd Event – Detail	Why #2 – Detail
3rd Event – Detail	Why #3 – Detail
How does it end?	How do you feel about this choice?

Prompt List for Grade 2 Focus: Me/My Friends/My Neighborhood/My School

First Semester: Prompts with Drawing

My Best Friends	The Best Pizza in the World
My Favorite Place	Show and Tell
Come to My House	My Neighborhood
Choosing the Best Pet	The Birthday Surprise
Recess!	My School
I Can Make It!	Crazy Creature in My Backyard

Name _____ Date _____

My Best Friends

Read the information in the box. Then do the drawing and writing activity.

Everyone has friends. They might be people you have met at school, in your neighborhood, or in your church. They might even be your relatives! Who are your friends? What do they look like? Why do you like them?

Draw a picture, and write a story about your best friends. Be sure to tell who they are, what they look like, and why you like them.

Pre-Drawing and Pre-Writing Activity

Here are some questions to help with your drawing and writing:

Who are your friends?
What do they look like?
Why do you like them?

Be sure to include details to make your drawing and writing interesting.

Your writing will be scored on how clearly you write and how well you get your ideas across in your picture. Be sure to check everything over before you turn it in.

My Favorite Place

Read the information in the box. Then do the drawing and writing activity.

Do you have a favorite place? You might find a place in your home, your yard, or some other place that is farther away. It might be a place you like to visit alone or with someone else.

Draw a picture, and write a story about your favorite place. Where is your favorite place? What do you like to do there? Why is it so special?

Pre-Drawing and Pre-Writing Activity

Here are some questions to help with your drawing and writing:

Where is your favorite place?
What do you like to do there?
Why is it so special to you?

Be sure to include details to make your drawing and writing interesting.

Your writing will be scored on how clearly you write and how well you get your ideas across in your picture. Be sure to check everything over before you turn it in.

Name _____ Date _____

Come to My House

Read the information in the box. Then do the drawing and writing activity.

> Would you like to come to my house? I would like you to see it. My address is _____. Now I am going to tell you what my house looks like so you can find it.
>
> Draw a picture, and write a story about your house. Where is your house? What does it look like? How can I tell it apart from the other houses on your street?

Pre-Drawing and Pre-Writing Activity

Here are some questions to help with your drawing and writing:

    Where is your house?
    What does it look like?
    How can I tell it apart from the others on your street?

Be sure to include details to make your drawing and writing interesting.

Your writing will be scored on how clearly you write and how well you get your ideas across in your picture. Be sure to check everything over before you turn it in.

Name _____   Date _____

Choosing the Best Pet

Read the information in the box. Then do the drawing and writing activity.

Your mom has just told you that you can have a pet. She takes you into the pet store, and there are SO MANY choices! She tells you that you should look them over, make a list, and then go home and think about it. Tomorrow you can go back to the store, buy your pet, and bring it home. Which pet will you choose? Give at least three reasons why you chose this pet.

Draw a picture of your new pet, and write a story about why you chose that pet.

Pre-Drawing and Pre-Writing Activity

Here are some questions to help with your drawing and writing:

Which pet did you choose?
Why?

Be sure to include details to make your drawing and writing interesting.

Your writing will be scored on how clearly you write and how well you get your ideas across in your picture. Be sure to check everything over before you turn it in.

Name _____ Date _____

Recess!

Read the information in the box. Then do the drawing and writing activity.

Every day you can hardly wait for recess to begin! There are so many things to do. With whom do you usually play? How do you spend your recess time? (play games, use your imagination, or play on the equipment) How do you feel about recess?

Draw a picture, and write a story about how you like to spend your recess.

Pre-Drawing and Pre-Writing Activity

Here are some questions to help with your drawing and writing:

  With whom do you usually play?
  How do you spend your time?
  How does recess make you feel?

Be sure to include details to make your drawing and writing interesting.

Your writing will be scored on how clearly you write and how well you get your ideas across in your picture. Be sure to check everything over before you turn it in.

Name _____ Date _____

I Can Make It!

Read the information in the box. Then do the drawing and writing activity.

It's fun to learn how to make new things. You might learn how to put something together, make something like an art project, or make a meal or a snack. What do you know how to make? What will you need for this project? How do you make it?

Draw a picture, and write a story about something you know how to make.

Pre-Drawing and Pre-Writing Activity

Here are some questions to help with your drawing and writing:

What do you know how to make?
What do you need for this project?
How do you make it?

Be sure to include details to make your drawing and writing interesting.

Your writing will be scored on how clearly you write and how well you get your ideas across in your picture. Be sure to check everything over before you turn it in.

Name _____ Date _____

The Best Pizza in the World

Read the information in the box. Then do the drawing and writing activity.

Almost everyone likes pizza. What's your favorite kind of pizza? Why do you like this kind best?

Draw a picture, and write a story about your favorite pizza.

Pre-Drawing and Pre-Writing Activity

Here are some questions to help with your drawing and writing:

What is your favorite kind of pizza?
Why do you like this kind best?

Be sure to include details to make your drawing and writing interesting.

Your writing will be scored on how clearly you write and how well you get your ideas across in your picture. Be sure to check everything over before you turn it in.

Name _____ Date _____

Show and Tell

Read the information in the box. Then do the drawing and writing activity.

Your class is having Show and Tell this Friday. On Show and Tell Day, you get to bring something from home and tell your friends all about it. What will you bring? What will you tell your friends about it?

Draw a picture, and write a story that tells what you will bring for Show and Tell.

What will you bring?
What will you say about it?
What will your friends think?

Pre-Drawing and Pre-Writing Activity

Here are some questions to help with your drawing and writing:

What will you bring?
What will you say about it?
What will your friends think?

Be sure to include details to make your drawing and writing interesting.

Your writing will be scored on how clearly you write and how well you get your ideas across in your picture. Be sure to check everything over before you turn it in.

My Neighborhood

Read the information in the box. Then do the drawing and writing activity.

> All neighborhoods are different. Some are quiet, while others are noisy. Some are fancy, while others are plain. Some are safe, while others are dangerous. Some are friendly, while others are not so friendly.
>
> Draw a picture, and write a story about your neighborhood. What does your neighborhood look like? Do you know any of your neighbors? How do you feel in your neighborhood?

Pre-Drawing and Pre-Writing Activity

Here are some questions to help with your drawing and writing:

   What does your neighborhood look like?
   Do you know any of your neighbors?
   How do you feel in your neighborhood?

Be sure to include details to make your drawing and writing interesting.

Your writing will be scored on how clearly you write and how well you get your ideas across in your picture. Be sure to check everything over before you turn it in.

The Birthday Surprise!

Read the information in the box. Then do the drawing and writing activity.

Today is your birthday and you receive a card in the mailbox. You tear open the envelope and inside you find a note saying:

"Happy Birthday!"
Here is a gift card worth $100 to go shopping at Kidworld.
You may spend it any way you wish!
Love, Grandma

Draw a picture, and write a story about your special trip to Kidworld. What will you buy with your gift card? Why did you make this choice? How will your special trip to Kidworld make you feel?

Pre-Drawing and Pre-Writing Activity

Here are some questions to help with your drawing and writing:

What will you buy?
Why?
How will you feel?
Be sure to include details to make your drawing and writing interesting.

Your writing will be scored on how clearly you write and how well you get your ideas across in your picture. Be sure to check everything over before you turn it in.

Name _____ Date _____

My School

Read the information in the box. Then do the drawing and writing activity.

> Every day you go to school. You go to school to learn things and to meet new people. What school do you go to? What is your school like?
>
> Draw a picture of your school, and tell what it is like. Include a lot of information to make your story interesting.

Pre-Drawing and Pre-Writing Activity

Here are some questions to help with your drawing and writing:

    What school do you go to?
    What is your school like?

Be sure to include details to make your drawing and writing interesting.

Your writing will be scored on how clearly you write and how well you get your ideas across in your picture. Be sure to check everything over before you turn it in.

Crazy Creature in My Backyard

Read the information in the box. Then do the drawing and writing activity.

Your class is writing a book called *Crazy Creatures*. Crazy creatures are make-believe animals that do silly crazy things. One night, you looked out your bedroom window and saw a crazy creature in your backyard. What did it look like? What was it doing? What will you do now?

Draw a picture and write a story about the crazy creature in your backyard.

What did it look like?
What silly things was it doing?
What will you do now?

Pre-Drawing and Pre-Writing Activity

Here are some questions to help with your drawing and writing:

What did the crazy creature look like?
What silly things was it doing?
What will you do now?

Be sure to include details to make your drawing and writing interesting.

Your writing will be scored on how clearly you write and how well you get your ideas across in your picture. Be sure to check everything over before you turn it in.

Second Semester: *Prompts without Drawing*

Remember:
The following writing tasks will be scored using The Simple 6™: A Writing Rubric for Kids (page 149)

The Best Book

A Special Person

What I Like About Weekends

Being a Good Friend

If I Could Fly

The Mysterious Box

When I Grow Up

The Winning Ticket

Only One Left

Helping Out

I Was SO Scared!

All About _____

The Best Book

Read the information in the box. Then do the writing activity.

Read any good books lately? Of course you have! Tell about a book you have read that you really like. What is the title of this book? What is the book about? Why do you like it so much?

Write a story about this book. Tell what it is about and why you really like it.

Pre-Writing Activity

Plan your writing on another sheet of paper before you begin.
Be sure your story has a beginning, middle, and end.
Here are some questions to help with your writing:

What is the title of this book?
What is this book about?
Why do you like it so much?

Include details to make your writing interesting.

Your writing will be scored on how clearly you write and how well you get your ideas across. Be sure to check everything over before you turn it in.

A Special Person

Read the information in the box. Then do the writing activity.

Your teacher is making a bulletin board about special people in real life. Of all the people you know, is there one person that stands out above the rest? Who is this person? What qualities make this person special? Why does this person mean so much to you?

Write a letter to this person telling them how you feel.

Pre-Writing Activity

Plan your writing on another sheet of paper before you begin.
Be sure your story has a beginning, middle, and end.
Here are some questions to help with your writing:

What is the title of this book?
What is this book about?
Why do you like it so much?

Include as many details as you can to make your writing interesting.

Your writing will be scored on how clearly you write and how well you get your ideas across. Be sure to check everything over before you turn it in.

Name _____ Date _____

What I Like About Weekends

Read the information in the box. Then do the writing activity.

After a long week at school, it is finally Friday! It's time to go home to start the weekend! How do you spend your time on the weekend? Do you have homework or chores to do? Do you look forward to special things on the weekend?

Write a story about what you like to do on the weekend. Be sure to include as many details as you can.

Pre-Writing Activity

Plan your writing on another sheet of paper before you begin.
Be sure your story has a beginning, middle, and end.
Here are some questions to help with your writing:

How do you spend your time on the weekend?
Do you have homework or chores to do?
Do you look forward to special things on the weekend?

Include specific details to make your writing interesting.

Your writing will be scored on how clearly you write and how well you get your ideas across. Be sure to check everything over before you turn it in.

Being a Good Friend

Read the information in the box. Then do the writing activity.

Friends are everywhere! They might live in your neighborhood. They might be in your class. Who are your friends? Why do you think they chose you as a friend? What makes you a good friend?

Write a story about why you are a good friend.

Pre-Writing Activity

Plan your writing on another sheet of paper before you begin.
Be sure your story has a beginning, middle, and end.
Here are some questions to help with your writing:

Who are your friends?
Why do you think they chose you as a friend?
What makes you a good friend?

Include as many details as you can to make your writing interesting.

Your writing will be scored on how clearly you write and how well you get your ideas across. Be sure to check everything over before you turn it in.

If I Could Fly. . .

Read the information in the box. Then do the writing activity.

Have you ever thought about what it might be like to fly? You could fly with wings, you could fly in an airplane, or you could fly in a helicopter. Which would you choose? What would you do if you could fly for one day? How would you feel at the end of the day?

Write a story about the day you could fly. Be sure to tell how you fly, what you would do, and how you would feel at the end of the day.

Pre-Writing Activity

Plan your writing on another sheet of paper before you begin.
Be sure your story has a beginning, middle, and end.
Here are some questions to help with your writing:

How would you fly?
What would you do?
How would you feel?

Be sure to include specific details to make your story interesting.

Your writing will be scored on how clearly you write and how well you get your ideas across. Be sure to check everything over before you turn it in.

Name _____ Date _____

The Mysterious Box

Read the information in the box. Then do the writing activity.

It is Friday the 13th, and you have always heard that Friday the 13th brings bad luck. So far, nothing bad has happened. You get home from school, come in the back door, and see a mysterious box on the kitchen table. What do you think it is? What will happen if you open it? What are you going to do?

Write a story about the mysterious box. Tell what you think is in it, what will happen if you open it, and what you plan to do.

Pre-Writing Activity

Plan your writing on another sheet of paper before you begin.
Be sure your story has a beginning, middle, and end.
Here are some questions to help with your writing:

What do you think is in the box?
What will happen if you open it?
What are you going to do?

Be sure to include details to make your writing interesting.

Your writing will be scored on how clearly you write and how well you get your ideas across. Be sure to check everything over before you turn it in.

When I Grow Up

Read the information in the box. Then do the writing activity.

Imagine yourself as an adult. You will need to have a job so you can support yourself and your family. What job would you like to have when you grow up? Why did you choose this job?

Write a story about your life as an adult. Tell all about the job you would like to have when you are grown up. Why did you choose this job?

Pre-Writing Activity

Plan your writing on another sheet of paper before you begin.
Be sure your story has a beginning, middle, and end.
Here are some questions to help with your writing:

Which job will you choose?
Why will you choose this job?

Be sure to include specific details to make your story interesting.

Your writing will be scored on how clearly you write and how well you get your ideas across. Be sure to check everything over before you turn it in.

The Winning Ticket

Read the information in the box. Then do the writing activity.

Details of an exciting contest are on the back of your cereal box. Winning tickets have been secretly placed in only ten boxes of Wheat Krisps. The ten people with the winning tickets will be contestants on the TV game show of their choice. You open the box, and sure enough, you have one of the winning tickets!

Write a story about the day you found the ticket. What game show will you choose? Why? Who will go with you?

Pre-Writing Activity

Plan your writing on another sheet of paper before you begin.
Be sure your story has a beginning, middle, and end.
Here are some questions to help with your writing:

Which game show will you choose?
Why?
Who will go with you?

Include specific details to make your story interesting.

Your writing will be scored on how clearly you write and how well you get your ideas across. Be sure to check everything over before you turn it in.

Name _____ Date _____

Only One Left!

Read the information in the box. Then do the writing activity.

You have finally saved enough money to buy a pet, so you take off for the pet store. You didn't realize they were going out of business, and there is only one pet left! What kind of pet was left? Will you buy it?

Now that you've decided, what will you do?

Pre-Writing Activity

Plan your writing on another sheet of paper before you begin.
Be sure your story has a beginning, middle, and end.
Here are some questions to help with your writing:

Which pet is left?
Will you buy it?
What will you do now?

Include specific details to make your writing interesting.

Your writing will be scored on how clearly you write and how well you get your ideas across. Be sure to check everything over before you turn it in.

Name _____ Date _____

Helping Out

Read the information in the box. Then do the writing activity.

Your grandmother recently fell down the steps and broke her hip. She lives on your block, so each day you stop there on your way home from school to help her out. What kinds of things can you do to help your grandmother? How do you feel about having to stop there every day? How does your grandmother show her appreciation?

Pre-Writing Activity

Plan your writing on another sheet of paper before you begin.
Be sure your story has a beginning, middle, and end.
Here are some questions to help with your writing:

What kinds of things will you do?
How do you feel about it?
How does your grandmother show her appreciation?

Include as many details as you can to make your writing interesting.

Your writing will be scored on how clearly you write and how well you get your ideas across. Be sure to check everything over before you turn it in.

I Was SO Scared!!!

Read the information in the box. Then do the writing activity.

Everyone is afraid of something. They might not tell everyone about it, but they are fearful of something. Has anything ever scared you? Did you fear for your life, or were you just a little bit scared?

Write a real or make-believe story about the day you were afraid of something. It might have been a big animal, a time you got lost, were locked out, fell in deep water, were trapped in something, or had a stranger chase you. Write a real or make-believe story about the day you were scared.

Pre-Writing Activity

Plan your writing on another sheet of paper before you begin.
Be sure your story has a beginning, middle, and end.
Here are some questions to help with your writing:

   What scared you?
   How did you feel?
   What did you do?

Include details to make your story seem real, even if you made it up.

Your writing will be scored on how clearly you write and how well you get your ideas across. Be sure to check everything over before you turn it in.

All About _____!!!

Read the information in the box. Then do the writing activity.

I enjoy having each of you in class this year. Even though we are together every day, I don't know everything about you. What are some of your favorite things? How do you spend your time away from school? What are you really like? What things do you want me to know about you?

Write a story that tells me things about you. I'm interested in knowing about your favorite things, what you do in your spare time, and anything else you want me to know.

Pre-Writing Activity

Plan your writing on another sheet of paper before you begin.
Be sure your story has a beginning, middle, and end.
Here are some questions to help with your writing:

What are your favorite things?
What do you do when you are away from school?
What are you really like?

Include details to make your writing interesting.

Your writing will be scored on how clearly you write and how well you get your ideas across. Be sure to check everything over before you turn it in.

Picture Book Resources

Aardema, Varna. (1981). *Bringing the rain to kapiti plain.* NY: Dial Books for Young Readers.

Ackerman, Karen. (1988). *Song and dance man.* Manchester, UK: Dragonfly Books.

Agell, Charlotte. (2000). *Up the mountain.* London: Dorling Kindersley.

Albert, Burton. (1996). *Journey of the nightly jaguar.* London: Simon & Schuster.

Aliki. (1998). (1998). *Painted words/spoken memories.* NY: Greenwillow Books.

Allard, Harry. (1977). *Miss nelson is missing.* Boston: Houghton Mifflin.

Allen, Pamela. (1988). *Who sank the boat?* NY: Putnam & Grosset Group.

Arnosky, Jim. (2002). *Turtle in the sea.* NY: G. P. Putnam's Sons.

Bagley, Pat. (1995). *Showdown at slickrock.* NY: Hyperion Books for Children.

Bahr, Mary. (1992). *The memory box.* Morton Grove, IL: Albert Whitman.

Bang, Molly. (1999). *When sophie gets angry—really, really angry. . .* Troy, MI: Blue Sky Press.

Barrett, Judi. (2001). *Things that are most in the world.* London: Aladdin.

Beaumont, Karen. (2005). *I ain't gonna paint no more!* NY: Harcourt.

Blonder, Ellen. (1994). *Noisy breakfast.* NY: Scholastic.

Blume, Judy. (1974). *The pain and the great one.* Manchester, UK: Dragonfly Books.

Brett, Jan. (1989). *The mitten.* NY: Scholastic, Inc.

Brown, Margaret Wise. (1949, 1977). *The important book.* NY: Harper Collins.

Brown, Margaret Wise. (1972). *The runaway bunny.* NY: Harper Collins.

Browne, Anthony. (2005). *My mom.* NY: Farrar, Straus, Giroux.

Cannon, Janell. (1997). *Verdi.* NY: Harcourt Brace.

Carle, Eric. (1987). *The tiny seed.* NY: Scholastic.

Charlip, Remy. (1964, 1993). *Fortunately.* London: Simon & Schuster.

Child, Lauren. (2001). *I am not sleepy and i will not go to bed.* Cambridge: Candlewick Press.

Child, Lauren. (2000). *I will never not ever eat a tomato.* Cambridge: Candlewick Press.

Cronin, Doreen. (2000). *Click, clack, moo cows that type.* NY: Simon & Schuster Books.

Cronin, Doreen. (2003). *Diary of a worm.* NY: Joanna Cotler Books.

Cuetara, Mittie. (1997). *Terrible teresa and other very short stories.* NY: Dutton Children's Books.

Curtis, Jamie Lee. (1993). *When i was little.* NY: Harper Collins.

Curtis, Jamie Lee. (2000). *Where do balloons go?* NY: Joanna Cotler Books.

Cuyler, Margery. (2004). *Please say please! penguin's guide to manners.* NY: Scholastic.

Day, Alexandra. (1991). *Frank and ernest.* NY: Scholastic.

Edwards, Pamela. (2001). *Warthogs paint: a messy color book.* NY: Harper & Row.

Fearnley, Jan. (2000). *Just like you.* Cambridge: Candlewick Press.

Fleming, Denise. (1993). *In the small, small pond. NY:* Henry Holt & Company.

Freedman, Claire. (2004). *Oops-a-daisy!* Wilton, CT: Tiger Tales.

Galloway, Ruth. (2001). *Fidgety fish.* NY: Tiger Tales.

Guarino, Deborah. (1989). *Is your mama a llama?* NY: Scholastic.

Hall, John. (2006). *How to get a gorilla out of your bathtub.* Lakeland, FL: White Stone Books.

Henrichs, Ann. (2006). *Synonyms and antonyms.* Eden Prairie, MN: Child's World, Inc.

Hurd, Thacher. (1984). *Mama don't allow: starring miles and the swamp band.* NY: Harper & Row.

Hutchins, Hazel. (2001). *One dark night.* NY: Viking.

Kellogg, Steven. (1985). *Chicken little.* NY: Morrow Junior Books

Kraus, Robert. (1971). *Leo the late bloomer.* NY: Harper Collins.

Lencek, Lena. (1994). *The antic alphabet.* San Francisco: Chronicle Books.

Lewis, Kim. (2002). *A quilt for baby.* Cambridge, MA: Candlewick Press.

MacDonald, Ross. (2003). *Achoo! bang! crash! the noisy alphabet.* NY: Roaring Brook Press.

MacLachlan. Patricia. (1982). *Mama one, mama two.* NY: Harper Collins.

Martin, Bill. (1967, 1995). *Brown bear, brown bear, what do you see?* NY: Henry Holt & Company.

Martin, Bill Jr. (2000). *Chicka chicka boom boom.* NY: Scholastic.

Martin, Bill and Archambault, John. (1988). *Listen to the rain.* NY: Henry Holt & Company.

Mayer, Mercer. (1968). *There's a nightmare in my closet.* NY: Dial Books.

McBratney, Sam. (1994). *Guess how much i love you?* Cambridge: Candlewick Press.

McGhee, Alison. (2004). Mrs. Watson wants your teeth.

McMullan, Jim. (2002). *I stink!* NY: Joanna Cotler Books.

McNaughton, Colin. (1994). *Suddenly!* NY: Harcourt Brace.

Moss, Miriam. (2002). *Scritch scratch.* London: Orchard Books.

Most, Bernard. (1990). *The cow that went oink.* NY: Harcourt Brace & Co.

Most, Bernard. (1980). *There's an ant in Anthony.* NY: Mulberry Paperback Books

Newman, Leslea. (2004). *The boy who cried fabulous.* Berkeley, CA: Tricycle Press.

Nixon, Joan Lowery. (1994). *When I am eight.* NY: Dial Books.

Noble, Trinka. (1980). *The day jimmy's boa ate the wash.* NY: Dial Books for Young Readers.

Numeroff, Laura. (1985).*If you give a mouse a cookie.* NY: Harper Collins.

O'Connor, Jane. (2006). *Fancy nancy.* NY: Harper Collins Publishers.

Older, Jules. (1997). *Cow.* Watertown, MA: Charlesbridge.

Older, Jules. (2004). *Pig.* Watertown, MA: Charlesbridge.

Park, Barbara. (1998). *Psssst! it's me. . .the bogeyman.* London: Aladdin.

Polacco, Patricia. (1994). *My rotten redheaded older brother.*

Pulver, Robin. (2003). *Punctuation takes a vacation.* NY: Holiday House.

Rey, H.A. (1941). *Curious george.* Boston: Houghton Mifflin.

Ringgold, Faith. (1991). *Tar beach.* NY: Scholastic.

Rosen, Michael J. (2000). *With a dog like that, a kid like me. . .* NY: Dial Books for Young Readers.

Ryan, Pam Munoz. (2001). *Hello ocean*. Watertown, MA: Talewinds.

Rylant, Cynthia. (1985). *The relatives came*. NY: Scholastic.

Sayre, April. (2001). *Crocodile listens*. NY: Greenwillow.

Schachner, Judy. (2003). *Skippyjon jones*. NY: Puffin Books.

Schulman, Lisa. (2002). *Old mac donald had a woodshop*. NY: Putnam's.

Sendak, Maurice. (1963). *Where the wild things are*. NY: Harper & Row.

Serfozo, Mary. (1990). *Rain talk*. London: Margaret K. Mc Elderry Books.

Shannon, David. (1998). *No, david!* Troy, MI: Blue Sky Press.

Silverstein, Shel. (1964). *The giving tree*. NY: Harper and Row.

Steen, Sandra and Susan. (2001). *Car wash*. NY: Putnam's.

Steig, William. (1982). *Doctor desoto*. Toronto: Collins Publishers.

Thomson, Sarah L. *Amazing snakes!* (2007) NY: Harper Collins

Van Allsburg, Chris. (1988). *Two bad ants*. NY: Houghton Mifflin.

Van Gogh, Vincent. (2005). *Vincent's colors*. San Francisco: Chronicle Books.

Viorst, Judith. (1978). *Alexander, who used to be rich last sunday*. NY: Simon & Schuster.

Viorst, Judith. (1991). *Alexander, who's not (do you hear me? i mean it!) going to move*. London: Aladdin.

Wiesner, David. (2001). *The three pigs*. NY: Houghton Mifflin.

Wiesner, David. (1992). *Tuesday*. NY: Clarion Books.

Willems, Mo. (2003). *Don't let the pigeon drive the bus!* NY: Hyperion Books for Children.

Willems, Mo. (2006). *Don't let the pigeon stay up late!* NY: Hyperion Books for Children.

Wood, Audrey. (1984). *The napping house*. NY: Harcourt Brace & Co.